MARKETING IN LIBRARIES AND INFORMATION CENTRES

MARKETING IN LIBRARIES AND INFORMATION CENTRES

S. Seetharama

Ess Ess Publications
New Delhi

Marketing in Libraries and Information Centres

ISBN: 978-81-7000-750-0

₹ 550/-

First Published 2015

Published by:
Ess Ess Publications
4831/24, Ansari Road,
Darya Ganj,
New Delhi-110 002.
INDIA
Phones: 23260807, 41563444
Fax: 41563334
E-mail: info@essessreference.com
www.essessreference.com

Cover Design by *Patch Creative Unit*

Printed and bound in India at Salasar Imaging Systems.

Dedicated

to

MY PARENTS

Contents

PREFACE

To say the theme "Marketing of Libraries and Information Centres" is a burning issue is stating the obvious. This is because Libraries and Information Centres were seen as conservative non-profit-making organisations with traditional values. But, this outlook seems to be changing due to the challenge of change - - - social, technological, economic and political changes - - - on the one hand, and the pressure of accountability and the emergence of enterprise culture on the other.

Further, information transfer and dissemination has been recognized as an essential element or input for all research and developmental activities in developing countries since a long time. Thus, libraries and information centers have been putting considerable efforts in the design of information services and products and in distributing the same efficiently and effectively.

However a lacuna exists in the transfer of information, especially in interdisciplinary areas. Increasingly, in recent times, R & D efforts have been mainly focused on problems encountered which require access to information that cuts across many disciplines. As an immediate response, new services and products were designed and developed. Ironically, however, the users felt that they were not being served adequately and appropriately. This led to an in-depth analysis which revealed, surprisingly, that the services were not user-oriented largely because of the non-involvement of users (in their design) and also that the extent of use made of these services was unknown to the generators of the information services! In other words, libraries and information centres instead of being "responsive" tended to become unresponsive organisations. This, perhaps, is true of many a library and information centre in this sub-continent. Probably, by designing and developing an appropriate marketing strategy, the situation could be altered and improved upon.

However, in the library and information centre environment, the function of marketing has long been overlooked. This is largely because some information managers felt that marketing is inimical to the nature of their activities. They don't seem to realise that marketing is essential to effective library management. Therefore, if libraries are to "survive" or to "thrive", the complete spectrum of marketing approaches becomes essential.

This book has been structured to cover all aspects of Marketing.Following the introduction to the subject of Marketing, the book focuses on 'Marketing of Information Sources' with particular reference to Marketing Concepts, Market Research & Market Segmentation, Marketing Mix components - - - namely, Product, Price, Place / Distribution - - -, Communication mix, namely, Public Relations, Advertising, Promotion. A presentation on Marketing in Digital Environment with particular reference to the Digital Marketing Mix, Customer Relationship Management and Digital Legislation is also included. Since the current slogan on everyone's lips is 'Self Sufficiency' and / or 'User Pays' principle and 'Profit-making', themes such as Costing & Pricing and Resource Generation have been extensively discussed.

A list of Bibliographical References, Indexes and Appendices containing Model Questions and a Glossary have been provided as it may be helpful for students.

This book is the outcome of experienced gained in teaching the subject as a course module at the Documentation Research and Training Centre, Bangalore and at various universities as well as in reviewing the literature on the subject. It is hoped that this book would facilitate librarians and information professionals to introduce and practice marketing in their respective institutions.

Hyderabad **S. Seetharama**

Chapter A
Introduction

1. PREAMBLE

Information transfer and dissemination has been recognized as an essential element or input for all research and developmental activities in developing countries since a long time. Thus, libraries and information centers have been putting considerable efforts in the design of information services and products and in distributing the same efficiently and effectively.

However a lacuna exists in the transfer of information, especially in interdisciplinary areas. Increasingly, in recent times, R & D efforts have been mainly focused on problems encountered which require access to information that cuts across many disciplines. As an immediate response, new services and products were designed and developed. Ironically, however, the users felt that they were not being served adequately and appropriately. This led to an in-depth analysis which revealed, surprisingly, that the services were not user-oriented largely because of the non-involvement of users (in their design) and also that the extent of use made of these services was unknown to the generators of the information services! In other words, libraries and information centres instead of being "responsive" tended to become unresponsive organisations. This, perhaps, is true of many a library and information centre in this sub-continent. Probably, by designing and developing an appropriate marketing strategy, the situation could be altered and improved upon.

In the library and information centre environment, the function of marketing has long been overlooked. This is largely because some information managers felt that marketing is inimical to the nature of their activities. They don't seem to realise that marketing is essential to effective library management. Therefore, if libraries are to "survive" or to "thrive", the complete spectrum of marketing approaches becomes essential.

Some of the reasons cited for the need for marketing are:

- Library and information Services are not highly used. (Pittsburgh study shows 7% of collection only used.)
- Justification of library and information centre expenditures getting difficult.
- Information services are not user-oriented.
- Little involvement of users in the design of services.
- Feedback on relevance of information services / products usually not available, and their evaluation not generally made.
- Information services do need professional selling.
- More effort is required in selling information than for tangible products.

2. DEFINITIONAL ANALYSIS

2.1. What Is Information?

While it is difficult to describe "information", perhaps it is easy to comprehend or understand. Conceptually, information has been described as a process, a record, a commodity, as input & output, as a resource, etc. As Saracevic & others have put it, that "no consensus as to the scope of the concept of information, let alone its definition has been reached."

For the purpose of our discussion, Information can be defined as *"some meaningful message recorded in conventional or non-conventional media and stored and processed by systems & services with a view to providing a more or less permanent memory of the messages and their dissemination to users"*. It is a diffused resource that enters into all activities and forms a component of all products and services that are sold. As McPherson puts it, "Information permeates all organizations; it is the raw material of cognitive activity . . . the means whereby organization obtains its window on the world". It is also paradoxical quality of being usable for measuring the value of other things, but not of itself.

BS 3527, Part I 1976 defines information as *"The meaning that a human assigns to data by means of conventions used in their presentation."* In other words, information is data that has been given shape. It may be considered as processed data. Thus information is data plus the meaning which has to be a result of human action.

An unconventional definition states that information is:

- What we take in from outside to feed our knowledge so that we can function successfully & achieve our aims
- What is necessary & what is available in a given situation for this purpose

Perry, on the other hand, remarks that "*information is theoretically any signal that can be transmitted & received, and as far as human beings are concerned, anything that can stimulate any of the senses is information. Information can be transmitted for the purpose of culture, leisure, work, research & everyday life.*"

Thus, any of the following categories can be included in the concept of information:

- Listings
- Bibliographical references
- References organized for information retrieval
- Information carrier or a copy thereof i.e. the actual book, journal titles, film, manuscript, database entry, etc.
- Advice . . . information that is interpreted & presented with appropriate experience to meet a specific application.

2.1.1. Types of Information

Information can be classified into different types using different characteristics:

By Source

- Signals -- Message in the form of signs, symbols, words & numbers
- Text matter -- carrying large amount of information as in reports, research articles.
- Graphics of various kinds like pictures, graphs, photographs.

By Channel as a carrier

- Literature -- primary, secondary, tertiary.
- Information institutions -- libraries, documentation centres, information analysis centres, etc.
- Distribution agencies -- book sellers, subscription agents, clearing houses

By Physical Media

- Oral -- Person to person, one to one, one to many.
- Recorded -- Paper print, Microforms, Audio visual, Electronic

By Recipient

- Individuals
- Groups
- Organisations & institutions

By Information needs

- By Standard
  - — Popular
  - — Scientific
  - — Technical
- By Type
  - — Know-why
  - — Know-how
  - — Show-how

Saracevic & Wood (1981) have summarized the breakdowns of information for developmental needs as follows:

1 In terms of information types
- — Scientific & Technical information
- — Policy & Management information
- — Operational & Industrial information

2. In terms of information use & transfer
- — Know – why – – more scientifically oriented
- — Know – how – – more technically oriented
- — Show – how – – more operationally oriented
- — Know – who – – more personally oriented

2.1.2. Use/Value of Information

Commenting on the value of information, Atherton (1977) remarks that the work of Researchers & Scientists necessitates effective communication:

- To stimulate thought & action by injection of & interaction with, other people's ideas, knowledge, experience, & achievements

- To promote continuous awareness of developments
- To diminish the probability of unwitting duplication of work
- To provide introductory & background information for work in unfamiliar fields
- To provide specific information & data needed for work at hand
- To meet specific requirements.

On the other hand, Saracevic & Wood identified the following uses / values / benefits of information:

- Decision-making / planning
- Problem-solving
- Knowledge, Competence
- Adaptation
- Productivity
- Efficient & effective use of resources
- Success
- Business
- Research & Development
- Education
- Self-fulfillment& advancement of individuals

2.2. Information as a Resource

On the other hand, Horton's excellent definition, which states that treating information as a resource means treating it as:

- Something of fundamental value, like money, capital goods, labour or raw materials.
- Something with specifiable & measurable characteristics, such as, method of collection, utilities & uses, a life cycle pattern with different attributes at each stage, & interchangeability with other resources.

- An input, which can be transferred into useful outputs.
- Something that presents to top management a variety of development choices, e.g. making trade off decisions between information-intensive & manpower-intensive investment . . . or between maintaining an information product or service in-house, or buying from an external source.

2.3. Information as a Commodity

Commodity has been defined as:

"A raw material or agricultural product that can be bought or sold, such as copper or coffee": a useful or valuable thing such as water or time" (New Oxford Dictionary of English.)

"An article or raw material that can be bought or sold, especially a product as opposed to a service", a "useful thing" (Concise Oxford Dictionary)

"An article of trade (in plural) goods, produce; profit, expediency, advantage, convenience or privilege (archaic). (Chamber's Dictionary).

In this context, none can argue against "idea of information is a useful thing". For purpose of this presentation, therefore, one can define commodity as an item that can be bought or sold. Under this definition, then the answer to the question posed in the title of this section would be "Yes, information is a commodity".

Nevertheless, the realization that information has become a commodity really dates back from the time information as opposed to financial & scientific data went online. While the purchase of a book or journal title gave virtually the purchase of rights in the information & ideas within that carrier for the whole of the time that it was in your possession, with online information one is presented with a possibility of a charge every time that you access information (Perry). Online services & electronic databases which are saleable are no doubt information commodities. It is worth mentioning, in this context, that while information is being bought & sold the world over, there is a lot of information that is available free for the users -- thanks to Internet, for example.

2.4. Information Transfer

The question then is .....What is information transfer? It is said to be a process by which a new idea or an innovation spreads among the members of a social system i.e. it is a type of communication process. It is the spread of the new idea from its source of invention, creation, or generation to its ultimate users or adopters i.e., to the destinations or recipients.

A study of the total information transfer process should normally consist of:

1. Identification of the points of generation & points of utilisation of information;
2. Identification of the sources / information transfer media / channels - - internal, external, formal, informal, documentary, non-documentary - - of information; and
3. Observation of the information seeking behaviour of information users.

This study would reveal a complete picture of activities involved in information transfer as shown below:

GENERATION → ACQUISITION → ORGANISATION & CONTROL → STORAGE → RETRIEVAL → DISSEMINATION → UTILISATION.

Generally speaking, information is generated due to activities performed by individuals or organizations as well as occurrence of events. Major information generators are R&D Institutions, Business & Industrial Institutions, Individuals, Governmental organizations at all levels - - central, state, district, etc. Apart from these institutions, other private & public organizations are involved in the generation of information.

In addition, events tend to be highlighted by media like newspapers, journals, television, radio, etc. and thereby media plays a dominant role in the generation of information. While all the above-mentioned institutions generate a considerable amount of primary information, thereby causing what is termed as 'information explosion / boom / bloom /flood , organizations like libraries, information centres, etc. produce a lot of secondary & tertiary information services and products to ensure accessibility of information to users.

While information is generated on a continuous basis, it causes difficulties to users who will have to scan & select relevant information from the vast quantities of information generated which involves considerable time and effort. Therefore, there is a need to link the users to information relevant to their needs - - a facilitating function. This role has been taken by traditional libraries & information centres like Documentation centres (INSDOC / NISCAIR, NASSDOC, NICFOS, NICLAI, NIACDAP, NICMAP, etc.), Information Analysis Centres, Data Centres, Referral Centres, Clearinghouses, etc.

2.5. Marketing

With the information world becoming increasingly competitive, marketing seems to have become the tail that wags the dog called information centre.The term "Marketing" means many things to many people. While to some it is selling, to others it is a promotional activity i.e., there seems to be a common misconception that promotional activities constitute marketing But in actual fact, it includes a whole gamut of activities, selling and promotion being part of these activities. This takes us on to the question "What is marketing?" While one sells cars, he markets transportation. In other words, in marketing, one looks at transportation needs, devises and offers a vehicle that will satisfy the need at an exchange rate that the market will bear or afford. Similarly, when one markets information services / products, it is presumed that he has identified the user's needs and devised a product that satisfies the needs at a price the user can pay in terms of money and / or time.

Perhaps, it can be said to be an exchange process where a user who has a resource to a non-profit information service obtains a document or information, the cost (of the service) being met by the user or the community through taxes. In other words, there is always a price to be paid whatever the context of the exchange.

While other definitions are given in library literature, the following seem to be realistic and pragmatic.

"Marketing is planning that focuses on products, place or mode of delivery, adjustment of cost / price to the market, and promotion to specifically targeted segments of the special libraries market (Zachert& Williams 1986)."

"Marketing takes the focus off the product and puts it on the users' needs. Products are developed from the users' point of view, not the producers. (Kotler et al 1977)

"Marketing is a stance and an attitude that focuses on meeting the needs of users. Marketing is a means of ensuring that libraries, librarians, and librarianship are integrated into both today and tomorrow emerging global culture. Marketing is not separate from good practice. It is good practice. (Smith, 1995)"

"Marketing can be summed as the process of customer-satisfaction engineering."(Smith, 1985)

"Marketing is about bringing them (users) in and bringing them back . . . [it's] a stance and an attitude that focuses on meeting the needs of users . . . Marketing is not separate from good practice. It is a good practice."(Patricia Fisher & Marseile M Pride).

"Marketing is a way of thinking which has to pervade the whole approach of the library staff. It has to do with predicting and providing services that people need and with providing services to the best quality." (Wakeham, 2004)

Thus, in an information context, marketing may be considered as a management philosophy whereby the organisation:

1 Actively **Monitors** the needs of its customers the users and non-users;

2 **Matches** itself and its products or service with identified customer needs so as to satisfy them;

3 Subsequently **Makes** itself known by communicating with customers; and

4 Finally, **Measures** customer's satisfaction in order to make any necessary adjustments. (Majaro, 1993)

In other words, marketing means adapting to the needs of the market and not foisting upon it a product thought to be useful to it.

Hence, it has been suggested that for libraries and information centres to be reasonably viable, they adopt the marketing approach, which, has substantially modified the traditional approach (See Table-1). While in the former, the emphasis is on the customer and the satisfaction of his or her needs, in the latter, it is the organisation itself or the existing product / services.

Table 1: Product-Oriented Approach and Marketing Approach.

Sr. No.	*Starting Point*	*Product-oriented approach*	*Marketing approach*
1.	Attitude to customers	Must be content with product	Information service must adjust to their needs.
2.	Approach to customers	Until customers turn up	Anticipate customer's wishes.

3.	Relationship with customers	Instrumental (as brief as possible)	Helpful and open-ended.
4.	Time required to obtain a service/product	Depends on technical services access	Depends on customer needs.
5.	Services/products supplied	Only what is available on the spot	Outward-looking network approach.
6.	Innovations	Chiefly designed to lower production costs	Aimed at providing better customer service.
7.	Attitude to services/ products	Information service supplies only what it produces	Information service endeavors to produce what it should be supplying.
8.	Evaluation of information needs	Restricted: Mainly in terms of printed matter	Broad: in terms of information (audio-visual)
9.	Feedback in relation to service provided	Mainly concerned with internal efficiency	Mainly in terms of effectiveness with regard to customers.

In short, the marketing approach suggested provides a manager the mental map to think systematically on the 5 Ps of any product or services – aptly called the "Marketing Mix", namely, – PATRON, PRODUCT, PRICE, PROMOTION, PLACE / DISTRIBUTION.

In addition, user education and evaluation are considered as key concepts in marketing.

2.5.1. Marketing of Information Services in India

The concept of marketing of information services and products in India can be said to be still in infancy. This is in spite of the fact that the Doyen of Library Science, Dr. S.R. Ranganathan had focused on the need for marketing (though, perhaps, he did not use the term) when he enunciated the Five Laws of Library Science in 1930. As a matter of fact, the Five Laws can be used for development of Marketing Principles in the context of libraries and information centres. This sad state of affairs may be attributable to the following reasons:

- Confusion at the conceptual level among librarians and information professionals that marketing is nothing but promotion and sales.
- Lack of definite marketing policy, end user policy, product policy, distribution policy, tariff policy, services policy at the national or local level.
- Users' needs assessment studies are inadequate due to methodological deficiencies and due to the fact that they are not carried out on a continuing basis.
- Lack of proper market research and segmentation studies.
- Product development and targeting leaves much to be desired due to the absence of market research and segmentation.
- Reluctance on the part of users to pay for information services resulting in adoption of economy measures. As a consequence, the physical quality and get-up of products are adversely affected.
- Evaluation of information services and products generated is conspicuous by its absence. (Gopalkrishnan, 1988).
- Marketing concepts are either not taught or least emphasized in library schools. In most cases, it does not form part of the curriculum.
- Information is a low priority item of users and the motivation to share even lower.
- Information consolidation activities / products, especially value-added products which are very useful to users are not generated to the extent needed.

2.6. Conspectus

Following the 'Introduction' in Chapter A, Chapter B focuses on 'Marketing of Information Sources' with particular reference to Marketing Concepts,Elements involved in Marketing, Marketing Programme, and Marketing Strategies. Chapter C deals with 'Market Research & Market Segmentation'.Chapter D,on the other hand, discusses the 'Marketing Mix' components, namely, Product, Price, Place / Distribution. Chapter E discusses Communication mix, namely, Public Relations, Advertising, and Promotion. A presentation on 'Marketing in Digital Environment' highlighting the Digital Marketing Mix, Customer Relationship Management and Digital Legislation follows in Chapter F. Since the current slogan on everyone's lips is 'Self Sufficiency' and / or 'User Pays' principle and 'Profit-making', Chapter G and Chapter H deal with "Costing and Pricing" and 'Resource Generation' (an important topic for libraries and information centres) respectively.

A list of Bibliographical References, Indexes and Appendices containing Model Questions and a Glossary has been provided as it may be helpful for students.

Chapter B
Marketing of Information Sources

1. MARKETING CONCEPTS

According to Jennifer Rowley (1994), the concept of marketing can be better understood if a few fundamental questions listed below are answered:

WHO

- are our customers?
- should our customers be?
- are our competitors?

WHAT

- new/existing products and services should be developed:
- new / existing markets should we enter?

WHERE

- should we develop?
- are our customers?
- should we distribute our products and services?
- are our competitors?

WHEN

- should we launch new products and services?
- should we enter / leave existing markets?

HOW

- should we promote our products and services?
- should we distribute our products and services?
- should we handle consumers reactions/ expectations?
- should we compete?
- should we maximise our returns?
- should we maintain our performance and evaluate new opportunities?

WHY should

- consumers buy our products and services?
- we develop new products and services?
- we remain in particular markets /business?

In short, the marketing approach suggested provides a manager the mental map to think systematically on the 5 Ps of any product or service – – aptly called the "Marketing Mix" – – which are PATRON, PRODUCT, PLACE / DISTRIBUTION, PRICE, and PROMOTION

In addition, user education and evaluation are key concepts in marketing.

1.1. Objectives of Marketing of Information Services & Products

On the basis of a definitional analysis of marketing, one can identify the following as objectives of marketing of information services and products:

1. To enhance use of information sources & services
2. To increase customer satisfaction

3. To generate resources for running the service
4. To facilitate production of user-oriented rather than producer-oriented products.
5. To help in the design, implementation and evaluation of the Marketing Programme.

The above objectives have been formulated so as to overcome the four barriers to adoption of marketing approach by information professionals, namely:

- **Attitudinal :** happy with satisfying a limited clientele, that too when asked for.
- **Structural :** staff coming in to contact with clientele are not information professionals and hence there is no staff to think from the point of view of the client.
- **Systemic :** library and information systems developed do not seem to allow the client or clients point of view inside the system
- **Environmental :** The culture, still believes in that information should be free.

In other words, the need of the hour is for information professionals to shift the emphasis from product-orientation to client orientation and adopt a marketing approach so that both provision and use of information is facilitated.

2. ELEMENTS INVOLVED IN MARKETING

The marketing of information services and products involves the following key marketing concepts:

- Market Research and Analysis
- Segmentation of the clientele
- Development (or adaptation)of products or services
- Costs and pricing
- Promotion
- User education

- Dissemination
- Evaluation of Products and Services (Saracevic & Wood,1981)

Echoing similar views, Zacharet and Williams (1986) have described marketing as a cyclical process comprising of the following five major steps, represented by five marketing concepts.

i) **Marketing Segmentation :** Identification of actual and potential markets and non-markets within the institution. Information gathering. Quantification.

ii) **Consumer Analysis :** Determination of needs and preferences. Information gathering .Quantification.

iii) **Market Positioning :** Prioritizing clients, groups and information service. Policymaking.

iv) **Marketing Program :** Determination of optimal mix of product, price, delivery mode (place), promotion. Planning. Customization. Coordination

v) **Market Audit :** Evaluation of plan and implementation. Information gathering. Quantification. Marketing judgements. Reporting

3. MARKETING PROGRAMME

Basically speaking, marketing approach would consist of identification of the target customers or user groups, determination of their information needs, designing of services/ products appropriate to their needs and at a fair price, choosing the right type of distribution channel after necessary promotional or advertising capacity, and last but not the least, feedback and evaluation of products and services. In other words, the steps involved in a marketing programme are:

Planning

- Market Research & Market Segmentation
- Product Development

- Promotion
- Distribution
- Pricing
- Evaluation

Implementation

- Review the Marketing Plan
- Schedule specification
- Resource Mobilisation
- Staff & User Education and Training
- Promotional activities
- Monitoring

Evaluation in relation to

- Objectives
- Products
- Performance
- Distribution channels

4. MARKETING STRATEGIES

While mission statement of an information service will answer the question of 'what business we are in?', but its implementation is via a set of strategies that will satisfy both long & short-term objectives. However, the essence of marketing strategy for libraries is to identify how they can best grow & become stronger in an increasingly competitive marketplace. But for this to happen, the librarians should continuously keep in mind Jennifer's questions (vide sec 1).

Marketing strategy, in its turn, is a written plan which combines product development, promotion, distribution, & pricing approach, and identifies the organisation's marketing goals. It determines the choice of target market segment, positioning, marketing mix, and allocation of resources. According to Amelia Kassel, basic marketing strategies include the following:

- Network, either in person or electronically, by participating in discussion groups online where your target markets congregate
- Direct marketing which involves sending out sales letters, capability brochures, flyers, etc.
- Advertise in print media or directories
- Devise training programmes that increase awareness about one's services
- Write articles for local media or professional journals and newsletters that describe the benefit of your service
- Direct or personal selling
- Send out publicity and press releases through local newspapers, radio a& TV stations
- Participate in trade shows at the local or regional level.

Institutions like libraries should choose appropriate strategies relating to management of product, price, promotion and distribution. While product management addresses user needs and wants through products and services and involves decisions relating to product variety, quality, design, features, etc., price management involves setting the price to different types of users, at different points of time, and includes price of products, discounts if any, payment period, etc. On the other hand, promotion management - - includes appropriate promotion tools & decisions on budget, objectives, message, specific media, and methods of evaluation of the promotional programme - -, and distribution management deal with distribution channels, transportation, etc.

4.1. Product and market strategies

The classic Product / Market Matrix (See Figure below) of Ansoff can be used as a framework for considering strategies as it aids the assessment of, and planning for growth potential. This can be modified and adopted by librarians to suit their purposes.

Fig. 1. Product / Market Matrix

	Current services / Products	**New Services / Products**
Current Markets	*Market Penetration*	*Service / Product development*
New Markets	*Market Development*	*Diversification*

Note:

a) Market penetration strategy is an examination of whether current users could be encouraged to make greater or more frequent use of existing services.

b) Market development strategy wherein current services are made attractive to clients who are different from the existing users.

c) Service development strategy is how existing services can be enhanced by new services and products.

d) Diversification strategy entails development of new services / products for new markets (new users / clientele).

4.2. Pricing Strategies

Major Pricing Strategies (*vide Chapter G*) that can be adopted are the following:

- Cost based pricing
- Demand based pricing
- Competition based pricing
- Marginal based pricing
- Dual pricing
- Subsidised pricing
- Profit based pricing

4.3. Promotion strategies

Strategies for Promotion include:

- Direct marketing
- Public Relations
- Advertising

(For details, please refer to Chapter E.)

Chapter C
MARKET RESEARCH AND MARKET SEGMENTATION

1. INTRODUCTION

According to Serraf, "Marketing is a coherent three pronged system of Research, Strategy and Action ... the purpose of which is to identify, anticipate, contact and monitor customers and to cope with changes and developments in the market." While strategy and action constitutes the "operational Phase" of marketing, research constitutes "functional Phase" involving the collection that will be used to establish the strategies and terms of action. In this stage, information about the market, customers and environment is collected. This can be construed as a pre-requisite for marketing and facilitates segmentation of the library or information center's market into smaller, more manageable groups that have like characteristics so as to design and develop appropriate services and products.

2. MARKETING RESEARCH

Marketing Research is useful for improving marketing decisions and understanding of marketing phenomena in any marketing situation. It is especially useful for Marketing of Library and Information Products and Services. It is essential to effective strategic planning and implementation and its consideration needs to be a continual process for most libraries and information services in the present complex and constantly changing world. The information generated by marketing research can be put to effective use in forecasting, planning, instructing and illuminating the whole management decision-making process (Rowley, 2001)

While Kotler (1982) defines that, "Marketing Research is the systematic design, collection, analysis and reporting of data and findings relevant to a specific marketing situation or problem facing an organisation", Green and others define "Marketing Research is the systematic and objective research for and analysis of information relevant to the identification and solution of any problem in the field of Marketing". In other words marketing research is a process whereby the information necessary for decision making in marketing is generated.

It is useful for improving marketing decisions and understanding of marketing phenomena in any marketing situation. The decisions to be made are: Identification and selection of marketing opportunities, design of marketing strategy for tapping the selected opportunity, design of marketing mix elements, i.e. Products, Price, Promotion and Distribution; and feedback & control of marketing effort.

Thus, marketing research is active and aim-oriented; it draws on statistics, psychology, sociology and anthropology. It looks at marketing mixes, pricing research, the effectiveness of advertising and investigates the whole of marketing communication.

2.1. Stages in Marketing Research

The stages in marketing research proper are the same as in the scientific approach and include:

1. Identification of the problem (for example: why does library use stagnate at round 20% of the population?

Which segments of the market make no use of databanks? Why not? How can a specific segment be reached?)

2. Review of Literature
3. Formulation of Objectives
4. Selection of Methodology
5. Data Collection
6. Data Analysis and Drafting Report

2.2. Types of Marketing Research

Perrin, Cheron and Zins identify three major types of marketing research: Exploratory, Causal and Descriptive (Figure 2). While Exploratory research is rarely conclusive and is associated with data-gathering methods which are cheap and relatively simple to apply like use of secondary data & case studies, the purpose of Causal research is to establish the cause effect relationship between the variables affecting a marketing situation and employs very sophisticated types of methodology including experimental methods and sophisticated statistical methods. On the other hand, Descriptive research is the commonest type of research in information services, particularly for the identification of customer

Fig. 2. Different Types of Marketing Research

- **Exploratory Research**
  - Secondary Data
  - Case Studies
- **Causal Research (Experimental)**
- **Descriptive Research**
  - Observation
  - Questionnaire
  - Diaries
  - Personal Interviews
  - Group Interviews
  - Telephone Interviews
  - By Correspondence

needs. In Descriptive research, the methods employed are : Observation, Questionnaire, Diary method, Personal & Group Interviews, Correspondence etc. Depending on the situation, these methods are used either singly or in combination.

3. MARKETING RESEARCH IN INFORMATION CONTEXT

Marketing research for information services involves the study of Communication and Behavioral patterns of the users and those to whom he has delegated his search. It is necessary that the research activity must continuously study the changing needs of users to avoid basing strategies on past, no longer applicable assumptions. Marketing research is especially applicable to answer questions about the basic elements of what marketing professionals have identified as the marketing mix – – Products, Promotion, Place, and Price. Research is necessary in each of these areas to maximize final acceptability and success of the information product.

While **Product research** is concerned with such elements as content, coverage, currency, format, frequency, graphics, packaging/repackaging, indexing and production capability; **Place Research** is concerned with existing distribution methods and the cost of alternative means of distribution of the product. On the other hand, while **Promotion Research** must determine (after considerable trial and error) the most effective means of promotion of products, **Price Research** requires complete data on the cost of production, basic financial policy and profitability goals of the organisation/library, competitive products and services etc.(Reed, 1992)

Marketing research, therefore, would involve the steps of data collection, data analysis, data interpretation, presentation of research, and feedback or follow-up (Ritchie, 1994). A diverse group of techniques and methods are appropriate and effective at each stage of Marketing Research.

4. MARKET SEGMENTATION

Market Segmentation is the segmentation of the clientele / users on the basis of the individual differences and group similarities. Essentially, segmentation is the division of the library or information center market into smaller, more manageable groups that have like characteristics. Marketing mixes can be fine-tuned to serve the needs of these groups or segments and marketing communications targeted more precisely. It is believed that the practice of segmenting markets would lead to better use of resources and services since those resources and service can be targeted with maximum effectiveness.

Paul Green and Donald Tull (1978) in their book *Research on Marketing Decisions* have set four criteria for market segmentation:

- Segments must exist in the environment (and not be a figment of anyone's imagination).
- Segments must be identifiable repeatedly and consistently.
- Segments must be reasonably stable over a period of time.
- One must be able to efficiently reach the segments through specifically targeted distribution and communication initiatives.

4.1. Characteristics of Segmentation

A market segment needs to satisfy the following criteria if it is to be targeted successfully:

- It should be **homogenous** i.e., the characteristic variables of the group need to be identifiable and strong enough to warrant different treatment.
- It should be **accessible** for targeting to succeed. An

identifiable segment may be available only at particular times, student populations in term-time, twilight shift workers, etc.

- The segment size should be **measurable** and justify targeting. This does not always mean large numbers but cost-effectiveness should be a primary question for librarians and information managers.
- Appropriate or natural segments will be identified as prime targets when there is a positive answer to the following questions
  - *Awareness* - - can they be made aware successfully?
  - *Availability* - - can the service be made available to them effectively?
  - *Affordability* - - can the segment afford to use the service?
  - *Acceptability* - - can the service be made more acceptable to them?

4.2. Methods of Segmentation

Market Segmentation involves the identification of the users (target groups) - - actual and potential, and their needs assessment. This would involve collection of information on the institutional projects and programmes as well as individual user's interests and needs.

In the designing of the user study, the objective of the study, the variables to be studied, the model to be followed, the population sample to be studied, the data collection methods to be adopted, the analytical methods to be followed are to be determined with care. In its turn, a study of clientele facilities the identification and analysis of their needs which may be categorized as functional / problemistic / social / emotional / epistemic needs. Another categorization would be for retrospective searches, current awareness, browsing, specific information, problem-solving, managerial decision-making etc.

While the methods of dividing the market into segments are many, it is often a combination of methods that leads to success. Segmentation can be by subject / institution / volume of use / age groups (adult, young, children, etc.) / special interest groups, such as, faculty, students and researchers. Ultimately the goals of Market Segmentation are to predict and influence customer or user behavior.

Markets can also be divided by:

- **Geographic Segmentation :** By Country, Region, State or City
- **Demographic Segmentation :** According to demographic segmentation variables such as age, sex, income, occupation, race, nationality, religion, education, family size and family life cycle stage (Bachelor stage, Newly married couples, Married couples with dependent children, Older couples with the head of household still working or retired, etc.)
- **Geodemographic Segmentation :** According to where they live (A classification of residential neighborhoods (ACORN System): Modern family housing, higher incomes, high status, non-family areas, Multi racial areas, Social class Grades: Upper middle class, Middle class, Lower middle class, Skilled working class, Working class, Pensioners).
- **Behavioural Segmantation :** Differentiates target markets according to usage rates, willingness to innovate or user perception of benefit.
- **Lifestyle Segmentation :** Attempts to profile a person's way of living and acting. VALS approach (**V**alues **and L**ifestyle **S**egmentation) classifies the population into a number of categories**: Sustainers**, who are disadvantaged but fighting hard to escape**; Belongers** who are conventional, nostalgic, and generally reluctant to experiment**; Achievers** who make things happen and enjoy life; **Societal**

conscious who have a marked sense of social responsibility.

- **Psychographic Segmentation :** is based on the practical applications of psychographics, wherein personal, psycho-graphical, social and cultural factors that govern user behavior are considered.

Thus Marketing Research and Segmentation study is a User Needs Assessment study with stress on economic aspects and constraints, as well as on alternate products or services. Table 2. gives a Market Segmentation of user groups and the services / products targeted to them. This is one of the essential and important steps in marketing as it facilitates in the development of an appropriate "Marketing Mix" for each audience or target market. The marketing mix deals with 4 "Ps" - - Products, Promotion, Price and Place - - together with the 5th "P" "Processing".

Table 2 : Market Segmentation: User segments vis-à-vis *Services & Products*

Services / Products	*Functional Groups*			
	(a)	*(b)*	*(c)*	*(d)*
Reference Services				
• Reader Guidance		x	x	x
• Ready Reference	x	x	x	x
• Literature search		x		
• Referral Service	x	x	x	
Current Awareness Services				
• Notification of current papers, etc		x		
• Research-in-progress bulletin		x	x	
• SDI	x	x	x	x
• Notification about conferences	x	x	x	
• Newspaper Clippings	x		x	
• Patents Information service	x	x	x	x
• Standards Information service		x	x	x
Condensation & Differential Presentation				
• Abstracts		x	x	

• Extracts	x	x	x	x
• Management Digest	x	x	x	
• Technical Digest		x	x	x
• Technical Note	x	x	x	x
• Product Information Bulletin (*in language*)			x	x
x				
• Process Information Bulletin (*in language*)			x	x
x				
• Commercial Intelligence Market Information	x		x	
• Forecasts & Trend notes	x	x	x	
• Company profiles	x			
• Notification of contracts & tenders	x		x	
• Environmental Scanning: Regulatory, Social, Economic, Technological	x	x	x	
• Technology Transfer Information	x	x		
• New Innovations		x	x	x
• MIS	x	x	x	
• Techno-economic surveys	x	x	x	x
• Data Service		x	x	x
• Information Analysis & Products thereof	x	x	x	
• State-of-the-art report &Trend report	x	x	x	x
• Critical compilations, etc	x	x	x	

Information packages **Small entrepreneurs**

COMMON SERVICES

- Translation
- Reprography
- Exhibition organization
- Editorial & Technical writing
- Preparation of charts, maps, etc
- Organisation of seminars, workshops, etc.

Note: (a) = Top Management, (b) = R & D, (c) = Middle Management, (d) = Technicians

4.3. Strategies for Market Segmentation

It is absolutely necessary that librarians identify those parts of the mass market, which they can most effectively serve. There are three strategies that can be adopted:

- Undifferentiated Marketing
- Differentiated Marketing
- Concentrated Marketing

4.3.1. Undifferentiated Marketing

In this type of marketing, all users have similar needs and the library caters to the whole group with standard services and products. In other words, those services and products, which appeal to broadest number of users, are provided. This strategy is resorted to when there are financial constraints and special services are to be curtailed

4.3.2. Differentiated Marketing

On the other hand, differentiated marketing is the dividing of the target market into smaller groups and designing of separate services and products for each group. In this strategy, the library recognizes the different needs of users and each individual group needs are examined and appropriate services are provided. Obviously, this approach involves additional staff costs, administrative and promotional costs.

4.3.3. Concentrated Marketing

Concentrated Marketing occurs when the library concentrates upon a small number of sub markets and provides in-depth services in a few areas thereby serving a small percentage of the market place. For example, a specialist library may decide to concentrate on Selective Dissemination of Information and High Speed Reference Service. In other words, prioritizing is resorted to among the users in provision of services.

Chapter D
MARKETING MIX

1. INTRODUCTION

Marketing Mix is the combination of product design, pricing, communication and distribution. It is the set of ingredients, which make up the Marketing Strategy, the aim of which is to maximize the satisfaction of customer needs. Each element in the mix is itself composed of sub-elements, which form a mix. There is, therefore, a "product mix", a "distribution mix", a "Communication" Mix (vide Chapter E) etc. The precise configuration of each of these elements and sub-elements will be worked out on the basis of the results of Marketing Research.

2. PRODUCT

One common mistake in marketing is to define the product too narrowly, which Levitt refers to as "Marketing Myopia" This is the reason why the term "Product" has been defined extensively. Product constitutes the heart of Marketing. The term "Product" refers to the overall output of an Organisation: goods, services and activities. It refers to both Tangible Physical Product (Car, Soap, and CD-ROM Containing Information) as well as Intangible Services (Insurance, Banking Products, etc.).

Chirouze defines the product from the marketing standpoint as a set of material and intangible elements fulfilling a practice and a prestige function, which the consumer wants for the services it provides and its capacity to satisfy needs.Levitt (1991) notes, "To a potential buyer, a product is a complex cluster of value satisfaction .... Customers attach value to a product in proportion to its perceived ability to help solve their problems or meet their needs"

Kotler (1994), on the other hand, has defined product as "Anything that can be offered to a market for attention, acquisition, use or consumption that might satisfy a want or a need." He distinguishes three levels in the concept of a Product:

1. Tangible Product : which is perceived directly by the customer? E.g.: Books or Physical Documents

2. Core Product : is the essential benefit obtained by the customer e.g. Information supplied by documentation centers, leisure activities provided by Public Libraries, Knowledge and Learning, which may be obtained by consulting a University Library.

3. Augmented Product : covers the advantages perceived by the customer who obtains or purchases a product, for example, the quality and objectivity of the information provided by a reputable documentation service.

Based on the information collected in Marketing Research & Segmentation, the management can take decisions on:

1. Who should be the user groups to whom the information services/products should be targeted to?
2. What should be the service/products that can be produced and marketed to the different target groups? Are there any alternatives?

2.1. Parameters in Product Design

Obviously in the planning, designing and

development of a product, the parameters to be considered are:

- Type of Library/Information Center
- Users and their Information Requirements
- Use put of the information accessed
- Purpose - - Stimulation, Knowledge, Current Awareness, Productivity, Theorising, Comparison, Problem Solving, Education, Decision-Making, Adaptation, etc.
- Periodicity
- Sources of Information (for generating the service/ product)
- Content Aspects - - Technical Sophistication, Temporal Aspects, Quality & Accuracy, Educational Qualities, etc.
- Presentation of Information - - Textual and Non-textual
- Format for Presentation
- Coverage/Scope - - Subject, Period
- Distribution / Audience
- Pricing & Promotion
- Manpower requirement - - Knowledge and Skill required, Number of Persons
- Technology - - Computer, Communication, Reprography and its Utilization
- Finance - - Revenue & Expenditure
- Managerial Considerations - - Feasibility, Phases of development, Cost (start-up, operational, reimbursable & non-reimbursable costs), Ease of availability of facilities, Manpower, Sources, Materials, etc., Length of Start-up time, Training required (if any), Extent of derangement of existing organisational structure, including displacement of personnel, etc.

Details regarding these parameters have been dealt with elsewhere (Seetharama, 1990). It is worthwhile mentioning that presentation of information in information products has not been given due attention. This has been aptly expressed by the statement "Presentation is the Cinderella of the information age". Perhaps, this is what Alvin Toeffler meant in "Third wave" when he remarked "many people feel cut off, because the very packages in which information arrives are unfamiliar... Therefore, a necessity has risen for adoption of innovative techniques for packaging, customizing and presenting information products to prospective customers or users of information. Information Consolidation & Repackaging is one such technique, since it plays a significant role in making available and accessible to users information that is appropriate to the task at hand and structured and packaged to coincide with his or her level, language and available time. Thus one can see the emphasis on customer satisfaction - - which is the major objective of marketing. Incidentally, this is in consonance with Blaise Cronin's definition that "Marketing can be summed as the process of Customer Satisfaction Engineering". Consequently, value-added information products are appearing on the information scene. This repackaging process has been further enhanced by the advances in information technology, particularly by the designing and development of appropriate software packages (Rath & Seetharama, 1990).

Therefore, while in the demand-driven approach, one most design and develop services and products required by the target group, in the supply-driven approach, efforts should be in the direction of ensuring a feedback from the users on the Information products and services. Some of the areas for feedback include : usefulness of products, ways in which information is applied by the users, ease of use, suitability of information supplied, suggestion for improvement. In other words,

Customer satisfaction, a key concept in the marketing approach should be the object of focus in the design and development of information service and products. Such an approach not only ensures provision of information in the right form at the right time, but also facilitates use of information. This is in conformity with the framework for information consolidation. .Thus, one can observe the process of information consolidation and repackaging as a marketing mechanism.

2.2. Lines and Ranges of Products in Information Services

It is necessary that information professionals must consider the Lines & Ranges of products, which are to be provided to the users. Line of products is the totality of products of a single type offered by a Library. Examples would be the various types of documents available from an information service: Monographs, Periodicals, Films, and Microfiches etc. The range of products comprises all the product lines offered by the organisation, for example, the various documents, customer services and research services. The figure below illustrates some possibilities for an information service:

Fig. 3. Lines and Ranges of Products in Information Services

Range of Documents	*Assistance for user*	*Research Service/Products*
Monographs	General guidance	Access to data banks
Periodicals	Reference & Information	Retrospective bibliographies
Maps/Plans	Specialised	SDI
Audio-Visual	Reference	

Informational professionals need to realize that products are not permanent and have a life cycle. They pass through various stages characterized by different levels of market acceptance. The stages / phases include:

- **Introduction Phase,** when the product unknown to public is introduced by special effort of advertising
- **Growth Phase,** during which the product achieves

a wider distribution. One feature of this stage is development of competition among same products produced by different Organisations.

- **Maturity Phase,** when the level of sales of product stabilises.
- **Decline Phase,** follows maturity phase when the product declines. At this stage, when new rival products appear, customer preferences alter and fashion changes. However, there is no definiteness in regard to the duration of each phase as well as the total lifecycle of any product. The implication is that even information products decline and die over time and need to be replaced by new innovative products appropriate to changing user needs.

2.3. Stages in the Creation of a Product

The creation of a new product is usually said to involve the following eight stages:

I. Search for Ideas : generation of many ideas with the aim of turning them into products or services.

II. Sifting the Ideas : collected for purpose of selecting the best of them.

III. Defining the concept of the product : with particular reference to content and form, the structure, method of indexing, interrogation and access facilities, mode of distribution, etc.

IV. Economic & Commercial Analysis : to determine the validity of the product.

V. Define the marketing strategy : to decide how it will combine with the other elements in the Mix

VI. Product Development

VII. Product Testing : for finding out the reaction of the users to the products

VIII. Product Launching

2.4. Products by Diffusion Stages

Perhaps, it is worthwhile here that one of the methods of targeting is adjusting the products to correspond to information needs at different stages of the diffusion process. **Saracevic & Wood (1981)** have given examples of products by diffusion stages in academic/research restitutions in the following table:

Table 3. Products by Diffusion Stages

Awareness	*Interest/ Knowledge*	*Attitude Formation*	*Trial Decision*	*Adoption / Confirmation*
Journal notices, Short announce-ment in professional news letters	State of the art report, Critical Reviews, Synthesized research results	Synthesis of critical reports & evaluations. Comparative results	Research data. Training/ Education Materials. Know-Why Information.	Continuing Synthesized SDI reports. Selective Current Contents

In addition, package media - - print, audio-visuals, demonstrations, interpersonal contact, etc. for the product also should be considered in marketing of information services and products. In other words in the design of information services and products:

1. The target user groups and the appropriate mix to be developed should be decided.
2. The existing infrastructure facilities available for the creation of the product have to be examined.
3. Planning individual information services and products taking into consideration the various parameters, including packaging and repackaging and naming of the product.

3. PLACE/DISTRIBUTION

Distribution has been defined by Lovelock and Weinberg as the various means available for providing customers with access to "The right product at the right time at the right place". Product distribution structures are, therefore, devised to match the habits and behavior of the groups of target customers. As a matter of fact, distribution is a matter of access over time. The service must be available when the customers need it.

Place is usually translated into "Distribution" in a commercial marketing mix, but suits admirably for libraries and information centers, since it refers to "Where" and "how" a service is made available to the users. The keyword is "Convenience" in the context of place and if one makes a service convenient and automatically the service use will grow. Since, if the point of access - - whether it is a geographic location or via a telecommunication network - - is convenient from the user's point of view, the service/product will be used and appreciated. One other factor, which is important, is "Accessibility". It is a well-known fact that availability does not guarantee accessibility.

This concept of "Accessibility" covers both "where" and "when". For example, opening and closing hours of a University Library are important. The library should kept open in the early morning as well as late evening hours to students/staff who would be attending academic programs/ courses the whole of the day and hence library becomes inaccessible during that time. It would be ideal if the library is accessible all the twenty-four hours in a day, but is rarely the case in a traditional library environment. However, in a network- based electronic environment, accessibility at all times is possible. But the user needs to be computer literate if he wants to enjoy 24-hour accessibility. In addition, the users need to be trained in using network-based services like Web and Intranet Services.

Another factor that affects "Distribution" is the environment as the user assesses the quality of the service on the basis of the environment in which it operates. However good a service may be, it tends not to be used if the environment is incompatible physically and mentally to the users.

Saracevic & Wood (1981) have identified the following major channels of dissemination/distribution:

1. Interpersonal Delivery : Products personally delivered either on the request or in anticipation of a need. This method is most costly and time-consuming, though it is very effective.

2. Group Personal Delivery : Products delivered to a whole group of users as at meetings, conferences, seminars, demonstrations, etc.

3. Strategic Placement : Products placed at strategic location frequented by users like canteen, sports complex, etc.

4. In House Dissemination : Reference and Referral

5. Local Depositories : Products through cooperative arrangements with an information system.

6. Mass Media : Dissemination through Newspapers, Professional Journals, Magazines, etc. Products to be in narrative style.

7. Broadcasting : Radio & Televisions

8. Mailing of products through postal facilities

9. Telephone

10. Computer Networks,etc.

In this step, the activities involved and decisions to be taken are as follows:

I. Identification of channels of distribution vis-à-vis the information service and product.

II. Choice of channel as well as type of level

III. Channel Performance Evaluation - - Marketing service output (volume of products delivered over a period of time), Cost and Efficiency and Innovativeness (ability of channel to adjust quickly and properly to changes).

While each channel has its own advantages and disadvantages, a judicious mix of different channels should be used for distribution of information product.

4. PRICE

The concept of price as an element of the marketing mix covers two different types of Price: the **Monetary Price,** which concerns the payment of certain sum by the customer/user, and the **Social Price** which corresponds to the additional effort which the customer must make in order to obtain access to a Product. As a matter of fact, the term "Price" is used to describe the market value assigned to an item. It is the real cost to the customer or user, including other costs than solely money. Price is ascribed value, generally expressed in terms of currency units, such as rupees, pounds and dollars. It may also be expressed in terms of services or other goods, which the seller and buyer may offer to exchange for the item. Price goes by many names - - Price (Most physical merchandise), Tuition (Education, e.g. College Course), Rent (A Place to live or the use of equipment for a specific time period), Interest (use of money), Fee (Professional Services: charged by Lawyers, Doctors, Consultants), Fare (Transportation, Air, Taxi, Bus).

Chapter E
COMMUNICATION MIX

1. INTRODUCTION

Once the library has identified the users and their needs and taken a decision on the line and range of products it can supply, success necessarily does not follow as the market has to be made aware of the services and products available. This is exactly what market communication does. Basically, market communication has been defined as "a series of techniques, often referred to as the communication mix, which make it possible to maintain systematic contact with market and thus to inform it about the products and services available." In spite of the fact that there is a certain degree of conceptual confusion regarding the term "marketing communication", most authors identify the components of the communication mix as advertising, public relations and promotional activities. (UNESCO, 1989)

Figure 4 shows how important it is for the fields of experience of the sender and the receiver to overlap if the message is to reach its target. This shared field of experience is essential in marketing communication. In other words, professional jargon should be avoided and words used commonly (by everyone) should be adopted, In essence, it means that the users' motives and habits should be understood in order to communicate properly with them.

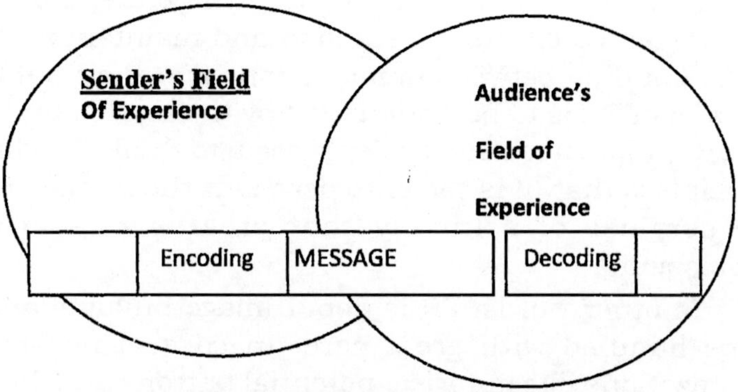

Fig. 4. Diagram of Marketing Communication.

The basic principle in marketing communication is the same as in any communication process and involves a sender, a message and a receiver.

2. PUBLIC RELATIONS

The term Public Relations (PR) covers the entire range of techniques for indirect communication with the market. PR is defined by the UK's Institute of PR as "The deliberate, planned and sustained efforts to establish and maintain mutual understanding between an organization and its publics." PR in libraries is more truly communication in that it is a two-way process depending on feedback in both directions and is a dialogue with the library community.

PR functions include: counseling based on understanding of human behavior; analyzing future trends and predicting their consequences; a search in public opinion, expectations and advising a necessary action, establishing and maintaining two-way communication based on truth and full information, preventing conflict and misunderstanding, promoting mutual respect and social responsibility. PR also has been defined as "a management tool function, of continuing and planned character through which public and private organizations and institutions seek to win and retain the understanding, sympathy, and support of those they are or they may be concerned "or" the deliberate, planned, and sustained efforts to establish and maintain mutual understanding between organizations and their publics. The aim of PR is to be understood by the market and not to manipulate it, as some people seem to think. The basic principle is that "it is easier to persuade the public to use the services of a library that creates a favorable impression."

In other words, PR is about image-building and is to be handled with great care. In case of non-profit organizations like libraries, potential patrons and donors are an important PR target. In regard to actual users or patrons, good PR helps in retaining their loyalty. Of course, for this purpose, managers wishing to ensure "visibility" of their libraries should adopt appropriate PR measures depending on the context -- briefings and press releases should be used to announce less important events such as those organized in public libraries. However, to get a good impact, PR communications should be precise, concise, meaningful and understandable by the target audience.

Apart from users, great care is needed in handling relations with administrative and political authorities on whom the information service depends for its very existence. In essence, in the information context, more importance to PR should be given than it has been given currently.

3. ADVERTISING

Advertising is the most visible component of marketing and is defined as the entire range of techniques for direct communication with the market. Unlike PR, which is a continuous process and an indirect communication, advertising adopts a direct approach and is a sporadic activity. The difference between advertising and public relations as ingredients in the communication mix is the level of control, which managers exact over the content of the message transmitted by these two channels. While the advertising message is determined directly by the organization, in PR the manager 'prepares the ground' for the communication (organizing events, press communiqués, etc.), but the final content of the message is beyond his control. (UNESCO, 1989).

Some of the common and relevant activities for librarians and information professionals under PR and Advertising (Kotler, 1994) are as follows:

Public Relations	***Advertising***
Press Kits	Print & Broadcast ads
Speeches	Packaging
Seminars	Packaging inserts
Annual reports	Motion pictures
Charitable donations	Brochures & booklets
Sponsorships	Posters & leaflets
Publications	Directories
Community Relations	Reprints of ads
Lobbying	Display signs
Identity media	Point –of –purchase displays
Company magazine	Audio-visuals
News (events / people / products)	Symbols & logos

(After Kotler, 1994).

3.1. Planning for Advertising

There are four stages in the planning of any effective piece of advertising:

- The setting of the objectives - - involves identification of the target customer, the required stimulus (to publicize a product or get consumers to like or buy it) and an exercise in quantification.
- The determination of the available budget
- Creation of the advertising message - - this is the

creative stage in advertising, which is divided into three phases

i) Select the concept behind the message

ii) The content

iii) Format.

(In regard to content, 2 basic questions to be asked are 1) what can the library and its information products offer to users, 2) what advantages can the user personally derive from the products)

- Selection of the medium or media most appropriate for the message. (On the spot distribution, postal delivery, door-to door delivery of leaflets or booklets; Badges, bookmarks, and other similar articles; Posters; Advertising in newspapers and journals; Radio and T.V. can reach a very wide public).

3.2. Checklist of Questions for Advertising

Gopinath (1998) has given the following set of questions which need to be considered while designing an advertisement:

1. Does the service or product have significant advantages as compared with alternative products capable of satisfying the same need?
   a) Who are the prospective users and what are their characteristics?
   b) What wants or needs is the information product capable of satisfying?
   c) Are these wants basic, such as, the desire to satisfy the information needs for improvement of career, profession, research / innovation?
2. Are there any characteristics of the product / service which if highlighted will motivate the client to buy?
3. Will underlying social and environmental conditions influence the demand of the product either favourably or unfavourably? Among such conditions

may be included:

a) Changes in field of research.

b) Changes in profit pursued.

c) Impact of technological developments.

d) Impact if institutional changes.

e) Impact of personal changes

f) Impact of political /economic changes.

4. Will the product encounter sales resistance on the part of prospective buyers because of the price of the product?

5. How much will an adequate program of advertising to consumers or users cost, for calculating cost-benefit analysis?

   a) During the first year?

   b) During a trial period?

6. How much sales of the generic types of information product be expected to increase as a result of advertising?

   a) The first year

   b) During a period long enough to provide a fair trial (3 to 5 years)

7. What share of the increases in the sales of the industry can advertiser expect to get during first year / trial period?

8. Will the extra gross margin resulting from the sales increase, cover the cost of the advertising program and make a contribution to a long range profit?

9. What feedback mechanism is provided to assess impact of advertisements for information products?

4. PROMOTION

The fourth P in marketing after Product, Price, and Place stands for Promotion, i.e. the communication activity.

The basic purposes of promotion are to:

- Attract and hold the attention of the clients (both potential and actual);
- Make the clients aware of the product or service and the organization providing it;
- Position the product or service and the organization in the minds of the potential clients in a unique and favorable manner;
- Motivate the clients to actually buy the product or service; and
- Constantly reinforce the message on the clients.

Pierce Levasseur defines promotion as follows "The purpose of promotional activities, which provide backing for the advertising campaign and the work of the sales force, is to stimulate the sales of goods or services by various means other than advertising or sales but drawing on both."

Promotion or 'marketing communication'

- is the key element to marketing
- must be clear and state what is being promoted, why and to whom and what the effect is
- is not synonymous with marketing in which significant data gathering and analysis is done
- is a tool of the overall strategy
- is campaign to communicate with a specific group of users about a specific service/resource (HINARI)

Promotion includes

- Institutional or Library websites
- Training workshops, seminars or meetings
- Direct mailing -- targets limited audience and personalized
- Advertisements, banners and posters -- attempts to reach a wide audience but with a simple message

- Leaflets and newsletters -- reaches a wide audience, can convey considerable information; limit to one topic
- Events -- reaches a wide audience; can convey considerable information and allows interaction between staff and users
- Word of mouth -- referrals by teachers or colleagues and library staff particularly with users. (WHO.)

Evaluation notes

- if the library or health information center has been successful in achieving the objectives of marketing
- confirms if the users' needs have been correctly identified and met
- measures performance objectives (data on institution's use)

Thus, Promotion involves mechanisms by which the target groups are informed about the resources available, services and products offered by the library / information center. Essentially, the purpose of promotional activities is said to be *to Communicate, to Convince, and to Compete.* Therefore, the promotional packages need to be so designed as to achieve these objectives. In this context, the information collected in the market segmentation stage would be useful. Some of the questions that need to be answered at this point of time are:

1) To whom are we addressing the promotional material;
2) What is the message sought to be communicated? Draw attention, provide information, persuasion?
3) What are the promotional mechanisms available? Which is the best? What are the alternatives?
4) What are the points to be considered in the design of promotional packages? What resources are necessary?

5) What is the role of the library staff in promotional activities?

It is believed that "word of mouth" campaigns are the best mechanisms for promoting the use of libraries. Alternate mechanisms include: Direct contact with target groups either by mail or in person; Indirect contacts through the medium of brochures pamphlets, posters, guides, handbooks, newspapers releases, tape-slide shows, video, radio transmissions etc., exhibitions and demonstrations, etc. It should, however, be remembered that promotional activity is not a one-time affair but is a continuous process. Further, while each mechanism has its own advantages, it would be ideal if different approaches were adopted at different points of time. Perhaps, the most effective way is through the library staff who should be courteous, efficient, and possessing the necessary knowledge and skill.

Some, however, believe that a very well-directed user education / information literacy programme (or user sensitizing programme, as is often referred to nowadays) will promote better utilization of the library. But sufficient care needs to be exercised in designing, developing and implementation of user education programmes.

Chapter F
Marketing in Digital Environment

1. INTRODUCTION

The transition of society from an economy based primarily on manufacturing to one that is predominantly based on information and the application of information and communication technologies (ICT) has profound implications, shaking the very foundations of traditional librarianship. This largely has been due to the paradigmatic shift of the library as a place...towards the information to which it can provide access to, "a natural consequence of the digital icon replacing the icon of books in modern times."

As a consequence, the digital environment is changing the functions of libraries and information services and the role of information professionals. In such a situation, marketing methods may change though the primary objective of marketing remains the same. Thus, the marketing model in the digital environment focuses on managing users' relationships and delivery & the appropriate marketing mix. In short, e-marketing and customer relationship marketing which are discussed here, seem to be the buzz words in the digital environment.

2. NEW ROLES OF LIBRARIANS AND INFORMATION PROFESSIONALS

Librarians and information professionals need to adopt digital technology for:

- Creating new products and services
- Retaining loyalty of individuals in those markets
- Supporting effective relationships with internal and external partners via intranets and extranets.

Therefore the role of information professionals is to adopt user-centric strategy, welcome new markets and new ways of reaching them and to encompass new products and services, and to create and deliver marketing messages in new ways as users will become much more active participants in marketing.

Bersson (1997) has identified the following new roles for libraries in 'a global network environment':

a) Internet access providers
b) Navigators
c) Educators
d) Publishers
e) Intermediaries
f) Information evaluators
g) Information organizers
h) Planners & policy makers

However, it is essential that information professionals work in the ambit of Ranganathan's Five Laws of Library Science as they are user-centric. As a matter of fact, they may be considered as marketing principles.

3. MARKETING IN DIGITAL ENVIRONMENT

The ever changing technological innovations have had an impact on library functions and services and have influenced library activities ranging from information capture, acquisition, organization, storage and dissemination of information to the clientele. Information services and products are now in multiple-formats giving rise to the electronic / digital library. In addition, it has put intense pressure from competitors like the database vendors and other private information centres and search engines. Further, the impact of Internet is posing a big challenge to the libraries as Google is organizing and making accessible information globally. Consequently, library is no longer the primary information provider as can be seen from the fact that users tend to focus first on Internet search engines for their information needs.

Marketing in the digital environment initially consist of:

- Exploring and identifying trends.
- Understanding market needs.
- Presenting appropriate marketing mixes and evaluating throughout.

The difference between traditional and digital marketing relates to the interactive nature of digital technology and in treating the user as a partner in the provision of services and getting inputs from the user in regard to the actual delivery of service that will suit his convenience and by a particular medium at a particular time and a particular quality level.

As a matter of fact, Kiani (1998) has shown the difference between traditional and digital marketing in the Table 4.

The goal of digital marketing is to make life easier for users by eliminating complexity for them.

3.1. Market Segmentation in the Digital Age

Segmentation is the process of creating groups of individuals (customers, Web site visitors, prospects, etc.) that have something in common. Segmentation's purpose is to make you, your marketing communications, your

Table 4. Traditional & Digital Marketing

Traditional Marketing	***Digital Marketing***
Mass -marketing	Individualized marketing or mass customization
Segmentation	Communities of the like minded
User as a target	User as a partner
Supply (to) user	Users demand
One to many communication	One to One Or Many to Many communications
Branding	Communication two-way
Monologue	Dialogue

Web site experience, your product offering, and so on more relevant to these different groups.

There are three main types of segmentation:

Demographic segmentation : based on *who someone is.* Demographic segmentation in online can also be useful. For example, "gender" can be a useful segmentation split because people can behave very differently online depending on whether they are male or female. So, to be able to segment your audience by gender, age, income, and more can be useful.

Behavioural segmentation : based on *what they do.* This segmentation approach is very popular in digital marketing because it's quite easy to understand how people behave thanks to the loads of available behavioural data. Again, it can be a very powerful technique to group people according to different behavioural criteria and to use that knowledge to improve the effectiveness of campaigns or to present different Web site experiences.

Attitudinal segmentation : based on *what they think.* Attitudinal segmentation is about getting into the minds of customers and understanding what makes them tick.

So, which type of segmentation is best? Well, of course, the answer is that "it depends." What problem are you trying to solve? What will you do with the segments when you've got them?

(Neil Mason, *http://www.clickz.com/author/profile1097/neil-mason).*

In this context, David Verkin's comment that "If you're on the wrong train, every stop is the wrong stop." aptly describes market segmentation in today's digital environment. A similar line of thinking can be seen when Eric Paquette, felt that market segmentation studies have been affected as content development has been influenced by the changing digital technologies. He believes that "a fundamental shift has occurred in how we communicate, entertain and learn that has massive implications for marketing strategy and marketing communications."

To quote Paquette: some common problems and associated implications with segmentation studies today include the following:

- *It is unclear which groups* represent *the biggest profit opportunities.*

  Marketing Implication: There is no guidance on whom to focus marketing efforts.

- *There is little insight into what will motivate each target to buy.*

  Marketing Implication : As a result, there is little help in defining your positioning and messaging strategy, and no assistance in identifying how to make the brand relevant, credible, superior and unique.

- *The various segments are more similar than different, particularly with respect to media exposure patterns. The targets can't be found in sales and media databases.*

  Marketing Implication : There's little insight into where to most effectively and efficiently market to these various segments.

  Consequently, three basic requirements to

successful segmentation and targeting strategy are:

1. Who is our most valuable target? Identifying your most valuable target helps define the focus of your marketing efforts. Today, measuring "valuable" has changed.

2. What are their needs, wants, and motivations? This information helps marketers define their positioning and messaging strategy so their brand can be relevant, credible, superior and unique. Today, this also encompasses the message you want your most valuable target to spread to others about your brand.

3. How and when do we find them? -- So we can advertise to them. This, of course, is critical in order to effectively advertise to them and so they can find your product or service. Today, it's also important that you reach them when they are most receptive and in ways they are receptive. It's all about "moments and mind-set".

He suggested that marketers take the following steps to make segmentation and targeting more effective in this new digital world.

1. Include measures of advocacy when assessing the value of segments and selecting a target.

2. Understand how your target behaves in the digital environment. As part of the segmentation, it's important to capture how your targets behave in the digital environment. What do they do online? On their mobile device? Are they "authors", "connectors", "commentators" or "spectators" in the digital world? "The digital behavioural composition of your target will guide what digital tools and website functionality your agencies need to provide,"

3. Determine where your target goes digitally. It's critical to understand the basics of where to find targets in the digital environment. How much time do they spend online and on their mobile devices? What websites do they visit? Where are they most engaged and most receptive? What types of mobile devices do they own? Where do they go on their mobile devices?

"Connect your target segment to the big media planning databases by including questions common to their survey and yours," Paquette suggested.

4. Understand how your target tries to find you. Where does your target frequently search? Do they use traditional search engines, YouTube, and social media? What keywords do they use when searching the category and your brand? It is not the same for all segments in the market. Do they prefer to learn about your brand from your website, social media, blogs, message boards or expert reviews?

All these questions need to be answered as part of, or a follow-up to the segmentation survey. Some of these points / questions seem to be relevant to libraries and information centres. Of course, they need to be modified if necessary. (Marketing Researchers November 2010).

On the other hand, according to Management Study Guide, the steps involved in Market Segmentation are:

- Identify the target market
- Identify expectations of Target Audience
- Create Subgroups
- Review the needs of the target audience
- Name your market Segment
- Marketing Strategies
- Review the behaviour
- Size of the Target Market

(*www.managementstudyguide.com/market-segmentation-steps.htm*)

3.2. Marketing Strategies in the Digital age

In attempting to discuss marketing strategies for

digital services, it is necessary to examine the nature of digital information services - -which are information and knowledge resources available in electronic forms including books, journals, CDs, videos, databases, films, audio products, etc. that are available through internet.

Some of the advantages of digital information services over print information services are listed below:

- Multiple access is allowed
- Continuous access at any time and place
- Instant delivery
- Saving of shelf space
- Prevention from damage, loss or theft
- No shipping and handling
- Access to out of print materials, etc.

Nevertheless, its drawbacks include:

- Cost of e-book readers
- Difficulty in accessing computers and Internet
- Resistance to change in reading habits
- Lack of knowledge of software / hardware (Ravichandran & Babu, 2008)

3.2.1. Developing a Marketing Strategy

Specific steps that can be followed in developing a marketing strategy are:

1. Define the products or services that an institution offers as well as their intentions. Determine how beneficial it is for your user / customer.
2. Establish a marketing plan of action for positioning your product in the market.
3. Develop a marketing study so as to determine the type of user /customer you are targeting with your service or product.
4. Study your competition to determine the various options available for your users to choose from.

5. Find out what sets your service or product apart from the competition.
6. Decide on a marketing budget and make sure your plan fits into it.
7. Determine the various marketing methods - -direct mail advertising, Internet marketing, and promotional events - - that you best can implement to promote your service / product.
8. Be prepared to modify the marketing strategy on a regular basis. (*http://www.wikihow.com/Develop-a-Marketing-Strategy*).

4. DIGITAL MARKETING MIX

The digital marketing mix consist of E-product, E-place, E-promotion, E-public relations and E-price.

4.1. E-Product

The service and products of a library are in the form of information in digital format. For example, Current awareness Services, Document Delivery Services, course materials in education sectors and product information in commercial sectors, user services via websites, such as, access to catalogues, etc. Services include: IT training; Education or work opportunity support; online access to national & local government policies, documents and debate.

While e-books have appeared, demand for hardcopy documents continues. Websites are e-products. They can function also as promotion devices to inform, persuade, entertain and advocate.

4.2. E-place

'Place' is also referred to as "Distribution" in a commercial marketing mix. It refers to where and how a service is made available to the users. This availability may be via telecommunication network. The keyword is convenience. Hence, a marketing mix for an educational institution often with a main campus library plus departmental libraries and collections would make a campus network to facilitate access to all services. Further, web and intranet services open up accessibility potential to a phenomenal degree

Virtual environment like the physical environment must reflect the identity and image of the service. It should be accessible from anywhere - - work space, student desk, home, etc.

Websites should be like supermarkets catering to different users' needs, they should be clear and simple to use. Good signposting and hyperlinks that allow a variety of routes to the required information help. Hence, website construction needs utmost care.

Data banks are another interesting example of the distribution of information products. They distribute their information through a system resembling distribution networks for physical goods. Data bank producers generally use an online host, usually a commercial organization which acts as a distributor for several databanks. With few exceptions, Online hosts have not so far merged to establish direct contact with their customers. They have been obliged to go through intermediaries who are either information brokers or in most case libraries (Arnold, 1987).

Distribution is also a matter of access over time and the service must be available when the customer needs it. University libraries, for example, must adopt opening hours that correspond to students work habits; Opening in the evening if necessary, and extending their hours during examination periods.

Technical and /or technological resources may be employed for the purpose of distribution. For example, the increasing use of telephone in information services has made distribution more efficient as the customer does not have to move around. Some American Public Libraries have set up an automatic 24-hour answering service.

The development of network and new technologies is bringing about considerable changes in the distribution parameters of information products; facsimile, electronic mail and even the use of satellites are now offering managers promising new methods for the distribution of information.

4.3. E-promotion

Apart from being an e-product, website can be considered as a marketing tool for the purpose of promotion when it becomes a shop window. Another and speedy option is Brochureware which is merely digitizing of existing promotional publications is best avoided since it ignores the nature of web user segments and is infuriating to the users who request further information offline and are presented yet again with the same information.

It is also desirable, if not essential, that the library's website message should be reinforced and also the URL must be on every piece of stationery, every delivery van, every internal and external notice board, every company or authority newsletter, on coasters in the coffee lounge and, of course, on every e-mail. (Desaez, 2002).

4.4. E-public relations

The internet, extranet and intranet offer numerous opportunities for dialogue and can be used efficiently and effectively as a marketing communication strategy. However, care should be exercised and interaction with users should be sought only if it can be maintained.

4.5. E-price

In the context of e-price, it should be remembered that cost to the user includes time spent at the site. User time, therefore, in all senses is an expensive commodity. In pricing, it is suggested that differential pricing for different segments of the market is adopted by libraries. The libraries need to offer their publications for sale via online charging & online credit facilities. Even in academic libraries, student and staff credit schemes need to be introduced.

5. CUSTOMER RELATIONSHIP MANAGEMENT

In the digital environment, libraries must add Relationship Marketing in particular, Customer Relationship Management (CRM) as another dimension in their marketing portfolio. While Relationship Marketing is about establishing, maintaining and enhancing contacts with users, suppliers and with distributions, CRM is "a holistic process of identifying, attracting, differentiating and retaining customers" (Strauss & Frost, 2001). They describe it as "participatory marketing, and share communication where everyone involved benefits from each other in an environment of mutual gain."

CRM strategy aims to identify:

- What users want?
- What to say to them?
- When to say it?
- What medium to use?
- How to gain their trust?
- How to retain their loyalty?

While information professionals have always been in contact with users, perhaps, the digital age is offering an opportunity to make them easier, faster and more effective from the individual user point of view. Since knowledge of user base, markets segmented to the level of the individual with help of digital technology, opportunities for capturing user data via digital technology, data mining potential for forecasting and planning are possible. Thus, the user can be interpreted into information product and service design and service delivery decisions, so that the relationship is mutually beneficial. (Desaez, 2002)

6. DIGITAL LEGISLATION

In the minefield of digital legislation, information professionals must pay special attention to:

- Data protection
- Outsourcing agreements
- Intellectual Property Rights
- Cyber Fraud
- Computer Misuse
- Domain Name Disputes
- Web- Advertising Issues
- E-mail and Internet Access Policies
- Online Content Provider issues, including defamation

It is absolutely necessary that librarians and information professionals in digital marketing to:

- Abide by data protection legislation.
- Seek the consent of the data subject (the user and permission marketing)
- Present clear and obvious advice on how information might be used and opt-out methods offered.

Chapter G
COSTING AND PRICING

1. INTRODUCTION

All organizations, irrespective of whether they are profit-making or non- profit making have certain goals or objectives which they seek to achieve in the most cost-efficient and cost-effective manner possible. This is because of the fact that financial constraints dominate effective functioning of any organization, and libraries and information centres are no exception to this rule. The difficulties encountered by service institutions like libraries is compounded by the fact that they cannot demonstrate tangible benefits as the production and manufacturing units of an industrial institution can. Thus, it becomes necessary for libraries to formulate clear cut objectives which would facilitate measuring and monitoring progress towards stated objectives. It is in this context that costing plays a dominant role by analyzing how the financial resources are being spent and also in pricing the services and products in the context of resource generation.

2. NEED FOR COSTING

The following are some of the factors / reasons that highlight the need for costing:

- Capitalization of Assets / Revenue

- Profitability
- Allocation of Resources
- Efficiency of Services
- Cost control
- Planning
- Pricing
- Managerial Decision-Making

2.1. Capitalization of Assets

The specific purpose of such a process is to create assets. Normally, it results in the creation of an asset. But, staff cost is not considered, usually, in a similar manner. However, in an industrial setting, the cost of labour is added as value on a product and the product is accordingly priced. In other words, it is suggested that in the libraries, the cost of staff in processing is to be added to the cost in relation to the book. For example, if the cost of the book is Rs 500, when it goes on the shelf, the processing cost of say, Rs 50 or 60 should be capitalized. The additional Rs 50 or 60 is the value added to the document. Therefore, if a book is lost, cost recovery should not only include the listed price of the book, but also the processing cost. It is for this purpose of capitalization that costing assumes significance.

2.2. Profitability

The concept of profitability should be focused on in the libraries in spite of the fact that they are considered non-profit making or service organizations. This is because they are hard hit when it comes to resource allocation or budgetary cuts. Libraries perform service function in addition to operational functions where benefits are not tangible. So, for the purpose of justification, one must think in terms of profit, say of an abstracting service. In these days where self-sufficiency is the slogan, one must try not only to recover the cost incurred for service given, but also make a profit however small it may be. One other advantage in costing would be that the library can forcefully argue for inclusion of library as a component of a Project Budget.

2.3. Allocation of Resources

In the allocation of resources to different information handling activities, cost information comes in handy. *(See sections 4 and 5).*

2.4. Efficiency of Services

The cost expended in regard to lending documents, abstracting, etc. may be indicators of the efficiency of the library, when one compares with similar costs in other libraries. Thus, cost element helps in comparison for efficiency.

2.5. Cost Control

If one contemplates for reducing expenditure by comparison with institutions, i.e. cost control, costing information is essential.

2.6. Planning

It would be like stating the obvious, if one talks about the usefulness of cost information in the context of planning libraries and information centres, especially, financial planning and management.

2.7. Pricing

The pricing of services and products, whatever may be the type of pricing adopted, the need for costing library and information handling operations assumes importance. In addition, pricing, perhaps, helps in knowing how much one is gaining or losing in providing a service.

2.8. Managerial Decision-Making

Managerial decisions as to whether to continue a

service / facility or drop it, whether to purchase or hire an equipment, whether to purchase one or two equipments, say, photocopiers, are largely facilitated by cost information, especially, in managerial decision on alternatives.

Examples:

a) Purchase or hire: For confidentiality, one copier may be purchased. For other purposes, one may hire a private party for photocopying services.

b) Abstract oneself or purchase an abstracting service.

3. CLASSIFICATION OF COSTS

In analyzing industrial information service costs, Armstrong (1972) has given the following checklist:

- Salaries
- *Salary burden* : additional costs incurred by the management on employees which includes National Health Insurance, Pension, Training board levy, Holidays and Sickness, Paid absence, Recruitment costs, Temporary staff, Canteen subsidy or luncheon vouchers, Group insurance, etc.
- *Occupancy costs* : Rent, Heating, Lighting, Cleaning, Dilapidations.
- *Department costs* : Stationery, Postage, Other staff, Telex, Telephone, Books, Journals, Travel, Consultants, Hotel and other expenses, Corporate subscriptions, professional fees, Training expenses, Conferences, etc.

The above costs can also be categorized broadly into Direct costs and Indirect costs. In a similar manner with little or no difference, other librarians have given their own checklist of costs. There is yet another categorization of costs resorted to by some and includes:

- Fixed / Variable costs
- Marginal cost

- Standard cost
- Opportunity cost

3.1. Fixed / Variable Costs

Fixed costs are those costs which are incurred irrespective of the level of activity. Eg. Salaries. On the other hand, variable costs are expenses incurred in relation to the number of items. Processing cost or Procurement cost is variable depending on the number of items. In other words, variable cost may be said to be the cost increase over and above the fixed cost. In this context, a pertinent concept to be mentioned is "Break-even" point, where no loss is incurred or where fixed cost is recovered.

For example:

100 copies cost Rs. 10,000

1000 copies cost Rs 15,000

i.e. Additional cost for 900 copies is only Rs 5000. Here, 100 copies is taken as a unit and the cost incurred is fixed cost irrespective of whether you produce 10 copies or 100 copies. The additional cost of Rs 5000 for 900 copies is the variable cost since it is dependent on the number of items. These costs have implications in the context of pricing services and products and the number of items to be produced. It is said that a pricing decision should at least be the fixed cost.

Thus, if one wants to price a copy at Rs 100, then the number of copies to be produced should be 100. On the other hand, if one wants to price it at Rs 50, then one should go for at least 200 copies to reach the "Break-even" point, where no loss is incurred and where fixed cost is recovered.

In other words, to determine the price and quantity of publication, it is necessary to know the fixed and variable costs and the "Break-even" point.

3.2. Marginal Cost

It is defined as the change in total costs of production which results when output is varied by one unit, or the avoidable costs of producing an additional unit of output. Thus, marginal cost is essentially a study of the effect of cost / volume /profit relationships based on a classification of costs as fixed or variable and can be incorporated into a system for recording and collection costs.

3.3. Standard Cost

It is based on a comparison of costs in relation to other organizations, and the main aim or purpose is to control and monitor costs. Standard costs are scientifically predetermined costs of materials, labor and overheads chargeable to a product or service. These are carefully computed and later contrasted with actual costs to aid in cost control. The difference between the actual costs and the predetermined standard costs are called variances. These variances are normally analysed by causes.

For example: In one library, lending of 100 documents costs Rs 50, and in another library it costs Rs 100 for lending the same. The question is, why the difference in cost - - may be due to inefficient equipment used (thus, one can replace), perks / incentives given to manpower, etc.?

3.4. Opportunity Cost

It is a cost concept which can be employed in decision-making. It is concerned with the best alternative foregone, and is usually measured by the profit foregone under the best available alternative. It is also called as Imputed costs, which is defined as the opportunity cost of inputs owned by an enterprise, which it supplies to itself and which have alternative uses i.e., a price or cost could be attributed to each unit supplied by the owner, even if no explicit price is paid. For example, Interest on an investment (say, an equipment) is an opportunity cost and should be included in costing of an information service or product.

4. HOW TO WORK OUT COSTS?

There are three methods which are applicable to Libraries and Information Centres. They are:

- Process costing
- Job costing
- Operations costing

4.1. Process Costing

This method involves the working out of costs of different processes and then that of the final output. In the context of a library, for example, the processes involved would be:

- Accessioning
- Technical processing
- Storing, etc.

All the above-mentioned processes involve costs pertaining to Materials, Manpower and Overheads. For example, in selection and ordering, costs are in relation to:

a) *Materials* : Book Selection Tools

b) *Manpower* : Persons involved in this process and may include the members of the Library Committee, if any

In a similar manner, the Material / Manpower / Overhead costs should have to be worked out in regard to Accessioning, Technical processing, etc. In this context, it may be noted that depreciation costs in regard to equipment / furniture have to be calculated.

The basic purpose of depreciation is to recover the cost on equipment by adding depreciation as a cost in the costing of a service. Computers, for example have a depreciation value of 33%.

In this context, if one assumes that it is Rs 4,50,000 for processing 10,000 documents, then the question is how to add the value-added cost (i.e. value added to the investment).

If the cost of 10,000 documents is Rs 50,00,000

Process cost	4,50.000
Total cost	54,50,000

(Note: This is Capitalization of Assets, vide sec 21.)

Therefore, Value-added cost is $\dfrac{4{,}50{,}000 \times 100}{50,\ 00{,}000}$

Hence, the recovering cost in case of loss of documents should include:

Actual + Value-added cost.

4.2. Job Costing

It is the costing for a specific or particular job / service / product.

For example : Current awareness bulletin, Abstracting service, etc. Here the costs are:

- *Material* : Core periodicals subscribed to a particular service (80% cost).
- *Manpower* : Cost in relation to Abstractor(s) Salary
- *Overheads* : Occupancy, Department costs, etc.

In this situation, the costs incurred up to the stage of manuscript preparation may be considered as fixed costs, and costs in regard to Printing and Publication of copies would be the variable costs. In costing the Current Awareness Bulletin or Abstracting service, the material cost need not be the journal cost as it may be taken as a process of asset creation. In such a situation, only the opportunity cost (interest on the investment) can be considered as Material cost while costing a service or a product.

4.3. Operations Costing

It deals with the cost in relation to operations. Lending is considered an operation. The cost elements involved include material, manpower and overheads. Generally, in the context of operations, one can ignore the material cost. Alternatively, opportunity and / or depreciation costs in regard to the concerned material may be considered. Manpower costs, however, need to be estimated. In regard to Overheads, a suggestion has been made that 80% of the overhead costs can be apportioned to the operations costing and 20% of the overhead costs to other services. Implicit in this suggestion for transfer to the concerned services costs, as operations performed are primarily meant for generation of services.

In order to arrive at unit costs per user or per transaction, it becomes necessary to divide the total cost by the number of users or number of transactions. For example, if the total cost is Rs 3,00,000 and the number of users is 500 and number of transactions is 10,000, then

$$\text{Cost per user} = \frac{3,00,000}{500} = \text{Rs } 600.$$

$$\text{Cost per Transaction} = \frac{3,00,000}{10,000} = \text{Rs } 30.$$

5. COSTING OF AN ABSTARCTING SERVICE: PPBS APPROACH

One of the methods developed for demonstrating cost-effectiveness of information services is Planning – Programming – Budgeting - System (PPBS).

The purpose of PPBS is to serve as a means of providing policy makers with an analytical evaluation of existing and proposed activities supported whenever possible with quantitative measures of performance - -

that is, with costing of library activities.

According to this approach, the components are:

- Objectives of the organization
- Activities (including, analysis of procedures) which relate to objectives
- Costs
- Benefits and Byproducts, and
- Analysis of alternatives, if any.

Ravichandra Rao (1974) has calculated the cost of an abstracting service using the PPBS approach.

6. PRICING

6.1. What Is Price?

A critical element in the marketing mix is "Price". The term 'Price' is used to describe the market value assigned to an item. It may be expressed in monetary terms or in terms of services or other goods which the seller and buyer may agree to exchange for the item. It may also be the amount of its accompanying services. (Vespry).

Price goes by many names (Kinnear & Bernhardt, 1986):

Price	: Most physical merchandise
Tuition	: Education
Rent	: Place to live
Interest	: Use of money
Fee	: Professional services charged by lawyers, doctors, etc.
Fare	: Transportation: air, bus, taxi.
Toll	: Use of road, bridge
Salary	: Work of Managers
Bribe	: Illegal actions

6.2. Pricing of Information Services

Pricing of information services and products is relatively a new concept. It has not been considered seriously since library and information services were provided "Free". But with increased emphasis on accountability and self-sufficiency in relation to resources, it has become necessary to cost the various activities and to recover costs as much as possible. Further, the fact that Information brokers and consultants are charging high fees for services provided and are thriving successfully is indicative of the users' willingness to pay for good products. At this point of time, it should not be forgotten that they are generating services using the "Free" materials/services provided for in the various libraries. On the other hand, it may be argued that since most libraries - - -public, academic, and special - - are supported either directly or indirectly by the Government (using the taxes received from the public), why should the end users be asked to pay. This is a question of ethics and hence not considered here. However, it should be remembered that not charging is also a pricing decision.

Pricing Objectives vary depending on circumstances:

1. *Token Pricing* : may be introduced, as free services are not valued; to educate users that information is not free ; as instructed by the supporting agency, etc.;
2. Income generation;
3. Sustainability;
4. To serve a target group; and
5. Profit.

Pricing of products should be based on costs incurred in the generation of a product or a service. This is not an easy process as whether overhead costs, depreciation, interest on capital, etc. should be included in costing is a difficult question to answer. But costing is a must, as it comes in handy at the time of budget justification, especially, if cost-benefits and cost-effectiveness can be highlighted.

Thus, to arrive at a pricing decision, the following questions need to be answered:

I. What are the costs involved in the generation of services and products? What factors/parameters need to be considered in arriving at costs? Which of these factors can be overlooked or ignored for costing and why?

II. Should the information services and products be given "Free" of charge? If so, to whom and why? What would be the impact in relation to value of product, if given free?

III. If the services/products are to be charged for, what should be the criteria for pricing? Full cost recovery? Partial or Marginal recovery? Should variable price based on the ability to pay by the user be considered? Should a profit percentage be added to the cost in pricing?

IV. Who should be charged - - internal or external clientele, or both? What would be the impact on users in relation to pricing of products? Would they be willing to pay? Would demand fall and to what extent if products are priced?

6.2.1. Product Pricing

Pricing is fluid, changing and rather uncertain as technology is changing the relative economics of traditional forms of publication against optical media, of use of online databases versus CD-ROMs, and so on. Pricing strategies to be adopted for information products can be determined through the consideration and inter-relation of three elements.

- Objectives of the particular service or product;

- Nature of the costs of the function and aims for cost recovery; and
- Nature / level of demand and the market.

On the other hand, a model of levels of information service was developed which has wider applicability and may be used to guide pricing. They are:

Level 1 : Advice concerning routine use of the library (Free, and free use of library of university if they wished to use it)

Level 2 : Quick reference queries, which can be handled, by reference to available resources within approximately 15 minutes time not charged.

Level 3 : Provision of information where the results are passed to the Organisation in the original format, e.g., online print out or photocopy of the original document, with annotations are appropriate based on direct changes, plus time factor

Level 4 : Provision of information where the results are reformatted to the organization's needs - - direct charges, plus much higher charge for time factor.

Level 5 : Provision of information where the results are presented with some interpretations or value judgment -- time charged, near management consultancy rates.

Level 6 : Acting as a consultant for Organisation on information management - - consultancy charge, based on hourly and daily rates.

Level 7 : Acting as a consultant for information strategy of a company, as in Level 6 above.

Level 8 : Acting as a management consultant, as 7, but higher rates (Brindley, 1993).

A similar line of thinking can be seen in Zais's pricing approaches and Merkulov's five pricing models. Clague (1992) has suggested the following guidelines on charging of information services:

a) Charge enough

b) Know what you want to achieve

c) Keep pricing structure simple and stick to it.

d) Identifying and Monitoring Expenditure

e) Setting fees

f) Maintaining the achievements of income goals

Thus the practical issues involved in charging fees for certain services include: setting the services, staff, determining the charges, legal aspects, market analysis, promotion and distribution of funds.

6.3. Major Pricing Strategies

In pricing of information services and products, formulation of pricing policy becomes essential. The pricing policy, in its turn, is dependent on the thinking of the management to recover costs, to make profit, to maintain standards of service, or a social objective of providing a service irrespective of the costs involved. Thus, depending on the pricing policy; one of the following approaches can be adopted:

Cost-based Pricing : Where the objective would be to attain a "Break-even" point where no loss is incurred or where fixed costs and variable costs are recovered.

Demand-based Pricing : Where as the name suggests, prices are based on the demand, i.e., lower prices where demand is weak and higher prices where demand is high, i.e., price distribution based on demand.

Competition-based Pricing : Where prices of products/services are based on what others are charging for a similar service or product, irrespective of the demand and costs incurred.

Marginal-based Pricing : Where the price is set to equal the marginal costs.

Dual Pricing : Where price is set on the basis of the paying capacity of the users.

Subsidised Pricing : Where price is set below the costs incurred more as a social objective

Profit-based Pricing : Where as the name suggests, the objective is to make a profit over and above the costs incurred

Strategic Pricing : Refers to the process of determining a price for services, based upon a thorough and sound investigation of all factors that comprise the environment: competition, market trends, customers, services, political, social, economic and legal determinants.

Zais's views that "Price setting is an art". But if information from models can aid the decision maker in the process of price formulation, then it should be explored and used are worth noting by Indian Librarian and Information Scientists.

Chapter H
Resource Generation in Libraries & Information Centres

1. INTRODUCTION

"Information is a resource whose generation consumes time and money, whose use conserves time and money, whose cost and value are not known to management". This statement succinctly sums up the situation encountered by libraries and information centres while making demands for funds from their respective managements. In addition, as libraries and information centres cannot demonstrate tangible benefits as the production and manufacturing units of a commercial organization, they are hard hit when it comes to valuable resource allocation. Perhaps, there is no library or information centre that has managed to escape the wrath of rising costs and shrinking budgets in recent times.

2. CHANGING FINANCIAL ENVIRONMENT

Since libraries and information centres were seen as conservative organisations with traditional values and time honoured practices, financial resources were virtually guaranteed for those operating in the public and academic sectors in the past. As a result, the library or its funding bodies rarely questioned the responsiveness of the library to the needs of the market place. However, some libraries have been responsive and innovative, but, as a group they have never been entrepreneurial. Fortunately for them, they were attached to public services or non-profit making organisations, which were themselves resistant to change and which fostered a traditional approach. Thus, activities in libraries were based upon budgets rather than being directly aligned to results and performance.

But, this outlook of libraries seems to be changing due to pressure from certain environmental factors. These pertain to the nature and provision of income or funds, and the changing perception of information and its use. To put it differently - - increased demand for services from users coupled with reduced government support has had an impact on the functioning of libraries. Thus, there is now, increasing pressure on librarians to deliver more with less! This situation is further complicated as information is now regarded as a commodity or as an organizational resource.

In other words, funding of libraries from traditional sources, such as, direct grants or subsidies from government and / or non-governmental sources is on the way out. Added to this is the government pressure for greater financial accountability on the one hand, and emphasis upon self-supporting and /or "User pays" principle on the other. Therefore, the need of the hour is for librarians to adopt innovation and entrepreneurship as keystones to change and for future success of libraries.

As a matter of fact, the restructuring of economy and the introduction of "self- financing" have become of utmost importance to libraries and information centres for their existence . . . nay, for their survival.

It has been reported, to cite an example, that self-financing has already been introduced by two central agricultural information centres in Hungary and the (former) USSR - - - AGRONIFORM and the All-Union institute for information and economic Research of the Agro-industrial Complex (AUIERAC). While the former had been working on a self-financing basis for the past few years, the latter had introduced it recently. Commenting, Mshveiidze has stated that economists have been drawn in as management staff in order to introduce cost accounting practices that would give the centres self-financing status. Costing of information and charging for information work have become priority considerations and he adds that a price list allowing upto 20% profit margin surcharge has been passed for in the (former) USSR.

In India, DSIR had suggested some time ago that information centres developed under NISSAT should become self-sufficient by generating their own income.

Financial resource generation in the information-based environment has come to stay, as can be witnessed from the fact that a number of commercial firm services and information brokers are successfully operating. Broadly speaking, information workers within libraries / information centres, institutions and private industry perform information services for fees charged to outside clients, or charged back to projects or departments inside the institution itself. On the other hand, entrepreneurial information brokers are self-employed or group of people organized as profit-making businesses. Perhaps, the librarian and information scientists can learn a thing or two from the information brokers who can extend the range of services that librarians can supply. They can provide specialized research skills, acquisitions, information and document delivery services, and help the librarian to discover new sources of information and to operate as a more dynamic information centre (Eibun, 1991).

Thus, one positive approach, in this context, for libraries and librarians is to think of income-earning or resource generation and / or cost recovery activities. This may not be easy, but, in the ultimate analysis it may be beneficial to the libraries and librarians.

Some of the benefits that would result would be:

- Spare capacity or resources (under-used collection and under- employed staff) can be effectively deployed;
- Income-earning by libraries would reverse the traditional poor image of libraries and librarians and consequently earn status and respect;
- Also would create a greater flexibility and a greater financial independence for the librarian than what he has today.

3. SCOPE FOR RESOURCE GENERATION

In an environment of dwindling resources coupled with increased demand for services from users, library managers will have no other alternative but to adopt both strategies for revenue earning and curtailing expenditure. However, in an effort to curtail expenditure, it may not be easy to abandon services or levy charges as there may be enormous exit barriers to some services on a social and economic scale. As a consequence, library managers may find themselves locked into many more programmes than they can afford! They will, therefore, need skills in politics, lobbying and negotiating in order to secure the necessary resources in a competitive environment (Jo Bryson, 1980). But, there is no escaping the fact that "revenue-earning or resource-generation in libraries" has come to stay. The question then is - - what is the scope and / or methods of income generation? At first sight, it seems to be rather difficult but with imaginative and innovative approaches, librarians have been able to raise resources, Table 5 lists potential and actual sources of income for academic libraries (Macartney).

Table 5. Sources of Income in libraries and information centres.

- Charges to Library Users
    * Fines
    * Lost books
    * Lost Tickets
- Sales to Library Users
    * Photocopies, Microfilm copies, Photocopies supplied for retention from external sources (in place of inter library loans), Examination papers, Binding, Typing, Withdrawn books, Withdrawn library furniture and equipment.
- Retail Sales to Library Users
    * Book-selling, Stationery, Audio-visual materials, Refreshments.
- Publications
    * Bibliographies, Newsletters, Course publications, Facsimile reproduction from the library's collections eg: rare books, Institutional press, Joint publishing ventures,
- Services to Faculties and other Internal Users
    * Computerised information retrieval searches, Photocopying service (Staffed)
- Services to External Users
    * External borrowers tickets, External membership (includes inter library loans, etc.) - - group membership, contact libraries, document supply, information and enquiring services, desk research and reports, consultancy, research, - - Management Contracts for other library services, Sale of space on Automated systems, Exhibitions, Short courses, Conferences.

- Charitable and related investments
  * Donations, Deposit, Collections, Endowments and Bequests
  * Sponsorship, "Friends of the Library".

4. COST RECOVERY PROGRAMMES

Thus with increasing emphasis on self-sufficiency in recent times, specialist and academic libraries would have to resort to cost recovery programmes.

However, when such programmes are instituted, careful consideration has to be given to:

- Pricing policies and price elasticity.
- Spreading the operating costs over a sufficiently large number of users, so that economy of scale may be working (Low fees over large number = Adequate revenues).
- Methods of Charging - - annual subscription, deposit accounts, vouchers bought in advance.
- Strictly controlling and minimizing internal expenditures and maximizing the efficiency of operations.
- Pooling of resources with other information systems; establishing a resources and operations sharing system.

5. PRICING OF INFORMATION PRODUCTS AND SERVICES

Pricing of products should be based on costs incurred in the generation of a product or a service. This is not an easy process as whether overhead costs, depreciation, interest on capital, etc., should be included in costing is a difficult question to answer. But, costing is a must as it comes in handy at the time of budget justification, especially, if cost-benefits and cost-effectiveness can be highlighted.

Thus, to arrive at a pricing decision, the following questions need to be answered:

- What are the costs involved in the generation of services and products? What factors / parameters need to be considered in arriving at costs? Which of these factors can be overlooked or ignored for costing and why?
- Should the information services / products be given "free" of charge? If so, to whom and why? What would be the impact in relation to the value of the product, if given free?
- If the services / products are to be charged for, what should be the criteria for pricing? Full cost-recovery? Partial or marginal recovery? Should variable price based on ability to pay by the users be considered? Should a profit percentage be added to the cost in pricing?
- Who should be charged - - internal or external clientele or both? What would be the impact on users in relation to pricing of products? Would they be willing to pay? Would demand fall and to what extent if products are priced? (Seetharama, 1990).

6. PRICING POLICIES

The development of effective pricing policies has become an issue of concern to both providers and consumers of information due to the rapidly increasing costs together with a political philosophy that favours privatization. In this context, five pricing models may be examined:

i. Optional pricing where substantial profits are made;

ii. Pricing according to value allowing both profit and loss;

iii. Full cost-recovery where all costs are recovered;

iv. Marginal cost pricing where subsidies are needed; and

v. Free distribution of services where full subsidies are needed (Merkulov, 1989).

A similar line of thinking can be seen in Zais' pricing approaches (vide Chapter G, Sec 6.3). In variance with these approaches, Levin suggests an alternative in the context of subscription price for CD-ROM databases - - namely, to price information services and products based on numbers and types of anticipated users, e.g. numbers of faculty; Ph.D. students; M.A. students; undergraduates plus and factor to take into account other users. Such a "Usership formula" is analogous to H.W. Wilson's established pricing policies.

While marketing information package products, costing should be worked out in detail, but, may not be the deciding factor in fixing price of the commodity.

7. CHARGING FEES

Some Guidelines given on charging for information services include:

- Charge enough
- Know what you want to achieve
- Keep pricing structure simple and stick to it
- Identifying and monitoring expenditure
- Setting fees
- Maintaining the achievements of income goals (Clague, 1991).

The practical issues involved in charging fees for certain services include - - setting the services; staff; determining the charges; legal aspects; market analysis and promotion; and disbursement of funds (Bath, 1989).

Nevertheless, it has been observed that charging for information services has been introduced, partially if not completely in Czechoslovakia, UK, USA, former USSR, Australia, Holland, etc. Further, charging IT-based services like database searching, online services and products has been rendered simple, thanks to built-in facilities.

8. IMPACT OF PRICING / CHARGING

At this juncture, it is pertinent to discuss the influence of charging for services. Advantages of charging include increased awareness of markets and users, the ability to maintain or expand useful services, and a more cost-conscious approach. Revenue generated from fees enables the library to purchase new equipments, recruit (temporary) staff, and to eliminate unnecessary requests. It also can be used as an indicator of the value of individual services. Problems include the need for new attitudes and skill, public sector constraints on staff number and consequential effects on the library and information systems. The introduction of fees can also result in a decrease in the interest in services as profit is not the main aim of library or information work and this may affect the principle of just access to information. At the same time, charging fees increases staff responsibility, resulting in higher earnings and increases staff interest in the implementation of progressive methods.

While such cost-recovery and revenue earning programmes have met with considerable success in developed countries, it may encounter some difficulties in developing countries like India. This is because of the fact that the users in developing countries cannot afford to pay cost-recovery prices and even the few who may afford will have problems in securing foreign exchange. This has been the experience of the Asian Institute of technology after nearly ten years of experience with its several specialized information analysis centres. It was found that they will probably never recover more than half of the operating costs (Brandeth, 1984).

Therefore, suggestions have been made for seeking finances:

- From donor agencies like IDRC, UNESCO, UNDP, etc. who support information handling activities.
- By creation of endowment fund and / or multi-donor fund.
- By tapping private sector.
- By including an information component in the budget of every research project, etc.

At this juncture, it would be appropriate to mention that viable financing of libraries cannot depend solely on direct subsidies or grants, or on a system of user charges, or on efficient operations and cost-sharing arrangements - - important as the last two are. There must be a careful balance of all these factors, depending on the individual situation. The most important and obvious criterion is how well the libraries meet their goals and how well they perform the services they were set up to provide (Atherton, 1977).

9. DEMANDS OF INCOME GENERATING SERVICES

While income-earning activities in libraries may not be difficult to introduce, certain factors need to be considered at the planning stage.

They are:

- Quality and Reliability of Library Services and Products.
- Calibre of Staff - - who must be able, hardworking and motivated.
- Impact on Users - - reaction from users to fee-based services which may result, for instance, delay in access to documents lent out.
- Impact on Library Staff - - some may be unhappy with a "commercial approach" in the library.

10. CASE STUDIES

The following are some Case Studies on Resource Generation presented at a Workshop at DRTC, Bangalore on the theme "Libraries and Information Centres as Profit-making institutions":

1. National Chemical Laboratory, Pune. The year-wise break-up of revenue generated (Rs. 59 lakhs) by providing information services and products during 1990-95 is:
   - Library consultation (Access to collection) : Rs. 8,61,211
   - Photocopy /Document delivery (in-house collection) Rs. 8,44,122
   - Photocopy/Document delivery (not in in-house collection) Rs. 2,06,595
   - Patent Information Services. Rs. 12,28,958
   - Translation. Rs. 4,19,941
   - Online services. Rs. 23,21,031
2. National Information Centre for Machine Tools and Production Engineering, Bangalore. The revenue generated by way of subscription to NICMAP services, Metalworking Abstracts, Photocopying service, Bibliographic reference service, SDI, Technical Enquiry service, Translation service for the period 1980 – 1995 was Rs. 52.33 lakhs.
3. Indian Institute of Science, Bangalore was able to generate a grand total of Rs. 4,28,834 for the period 1991-95.
4. British Council Libraries in India was able to generate revenue through membership subscription, overdue charges, inter-library loan, membership forms, sale of withdrawn books, photocopying, reservation, on-line searching, BLDSA/BMA commission, Sponsorships, Contents page service, CD ROM searches, Sale of publications, Consultancy fee, fee for organizing programmes, etc. Out of the many sources, the main source contributing about 84% of the revenue is

the membership fees. (515,000 pounds for 1991-2). Another method adopted for conservation of valuable financial resources was by expenditure management. For example, it was found that a shocking figure of 20% expenditure on "medical collections" which was equal to almost 200,000 pounds and this did not correlate favourably with membership percentages and use pattern. This anomaly was corrected subsequently. Thus, apart from traditional skills in information management, but also financial management, especially, ability to reduce costs, and increase revenue.

5. INSDOC. Delhi was able to generate revenue from its services, from sponsored / consultancy projects.

   The comparative statement of external cash flow (in lakhs) at INSDOC was:

Year	From services	From sponsored/ consultancy projects	Total
1991-2	25.95	10.144	36.094
1992-3	31.811	13.372	45.183
1993-4	72.563	105.458	178.021

6. National Information Centre for Textile and Allied Subjects (NICTAS), Ahmedabad was able to generate revenue to the tune of Rs. 29,91,023 for the period 1986 to 1995 through the sale of its information services and products.

7. Harsha Parekh discusses the objectives and processes involved in producing and marketing information packages for meeting day-to-day living information needs of women. She relates the SNDT Women's University Library experience.

8. Arpana and others discuss the procedure for costing and pricing information packages on AIDS, Child Abuse and Legal information for women.

9. Vaishnav and Bapat (1998) discuss the costing of a SDI service.

10. Madhuri Naik and Harsha Parekh discuss the market demand for electronic information products and outline the methodology of costing and pricing electronic information products.

    Thus, one can see that efforts are being made by libraries and librarians to generate financial resources.

11. CONCLUDING REMARKS

From the foregoing account, it becomes clear that due to reduced financial support on the one hand, and increased demand for services from the users on the other, some types of library services and products will be charged for in the future to overcome the financial stringent conditions. In addition, librarians will have to resort to other resource generating mechanisms. But, this would mean that libraries adopt innovative and imaginative approaches in the design and development of services and products so that the users would not only be attracted to them, but also be willing to pay for services received. Of course, willingness to pay would depend on the quality and reliability of the services and products. In addition, it is absolutely necessary that information professionals and the libraries / information centres employing them should design and develop appropriate marketing strategies - - which relate to product, price, promotion, placement / distribution and called "marketing mix". It is only then one can expect better utilization of information services and products generated by libraries and information centres. In turn, this would facilitate income / resource generation.

But, the librarians need to possess knowledge and skill for adapting and adopting particular approaches for particular activities. They should be creative, entrepreneurial, motivated, risk-taking, and ready to accept change so as to champion their cause in an open environment where competition between groups for scarce resource exists. This competition, in its turn, would result in improved performance of the library. At the same time, when libraries generate resources, their image changes and this in turn will earn status and respect for libraries and librarians.

EPILOGUE

Thus, the challenge of change, the pressure for accountability, and the emergence of enterprise culture emphasise the fact that libraries and information centres should be proactive rather than passive and reactive. Library and Information professionals, in their turn, should be aware of the importance of the economic prosperity of the organization and work for it. They should seek ways of improving the standard of information services under market economy conditions. Perhaps, librarians & information professionals should peruse the Guidelines developed by ASTINFO (1983) for Marketing of Information Services and Products (See Appendix) as it would stand them in good stead in developing their own Marketing Programmes They should determine which products users require, their quality and features and prices they can be sold.

Finally, if libraries and information centres and librarians / information professionals have to exist and survive in the future, they need to be *conservative in spending and aggressive in marketing,* particularly, in selling their services and products so as to generate the necessary financial resources, In other words, self-sufficiency in finances initially, followed by profit-making should be the goal. Thus, *"Earn or Exit" or "Earn or become Extinct"* seems to be the message for the libraries and librarians. However, in this commercial approach, the objectives and ideals of libraries and information centres should not be forgotten.

References and Further Reading

1. **ARNOLDS (SE):** "End-users: Dreams or Dollars." (Online.11; 1987; 71-8)
2. **ATHERTON (Pauline):** Handbook for information Systems and Services. 1977, UNESCO, Paris.
3. **BATH (Anne):** Introducing entrepreneurial service in publicly funded libraries: A review. (*In* Health information: New directions. Proceedings of the joint conference of the Health Libraries Sections of the Australian Library & information Association. 1989; 157-63).
4. **BENSON (AC):** Neal-Schuman complete internet companion for librarians.1997.Neal-Schuman.
5. **BRANDRETH (M) :** Specialised information Analysis centre, *In* International Development: Report of a meeting held in 1982. IDRC Manuscript Reports Series. March 1984.
6. **BRINDLEY (LJ):** Information service and Information product pricing. (Aslib proc.45; 1993; 297-305)
7. **BRYSON (J O):** Effective library and information centre management.1980, Gower Publishing Company, USA.
8. **CLAGUE (Leslie):** Charging for information services. (New Zealand Libraries. 46, 9; 1991; 16-17).
9. **CRONIN (B):** Marketing of Library & Information Services, 1981. ASLIB. London.
10. **DESAEF (EE):** Marketing concepts for libraries and information services.
11. **EIBLUN (P):** The Broker: An integral part of the information chain. (Information Today, 8, 9; 1991; 16-17).

12. **GREEN (Paul) and TULL (Donald):** Research on Marketing Decisions, (1978)*Quoted in:* NEAL (William D). Principles of Market Segmentation.(www.mktgsensei.com/.../ **Segmentation/Principles**%20of%20**Market**%20**S**...)

13. **KIANI (G).** Marketing opportunities in the digital world (Internet Research: Electronic Networking Applications and policy.8, 2; 1998; 185-194)

14. **KOTLER (P)** Marketing for Non-Profit Organisation Ed 2. 1982- Englewood cliffs. New Jersey. Prentice- Hall.

15. **MACARTNEY (N).** Revenue earning and cost recovery.

16. **MAJARO (S)** The essence of marketing. 1993. Englewood cliffs. New Jersey. Prentice- Hall.

17. **MERKALOV (GG):** Problems of financing special libraries in the conditions of budget control. (Nauchaye I tekhnicheskie Biblioteki SSSR. 1,3; 1990; 2-11).

18. **MSHVELIDZE (AI):** Establishment for STI: Their problems with self-finance. (Nauchoro Tekhnicheskaya Informataiya, Series, 1, 3, 1990; 2-11).

19. **RAVICHANDRA RAO (I K).** Planning and Costing of a Local Abstracting Periodical. (DRTC Seminar. 11; 1974; Paper C).

20. **ROWLEY (J):**Information Marketing in a Digital World. (Library Hi Tech 20, 3; 2002; 352-8)

21. **SARACEVIC (T) and WOOD (J S)**:Consolidation of Information: A Handbook of Evaluation, Restructuring, Repackaging of Scientific and Technical Information. 1982, UNESCO. Paris

22. **SEETHARAMA (S).** Costing of Information Systems and Services: Some general considerations. (DRTC Annual Seminar. 1990; Paper CB).

23. **SEETHARAMA (S):** Guidelines for Planning of Libraries and Information Centres. 1990. IASLIC, Kolkata.

24. **SEETHARAMA (S):** Information Consolidation and Packaging. 1997. Ess Ess Publications, New Delhi.

25. **SEETHARAMA (S):**Information Marketing: A new dimension in Library &Information Science (In Probir Raychoudhary and Nirmalendu Mukhopadhyay, Library & Information Services in India. (Dr.S.N.Ganguly Commemoration Volume). Kolkata.IASLIC.2000 p213-232).

26. **SEETHARAMA (S)**, *Ed.* Libraries and Information Centres

as Profit-making Institutions. 1998, Ess Ess Publications, New Delhi.

27. **STRAUSS (J).**E-marketing. Edn.2. Prentice-Hall.

28. **UNESCO:** Workshop on Marketing of Information Products and Services. 27th Nov-1st Dec 1989. New Delhi.

29. **WAKEHAM M.** Marketing and health libraries. Health Information and Libraries Journal:December 2004:21(4) : 237-46

30. **WHO:** Marketing Strategies for the Use of HINARI

31. **ZACHERT (NJ) & WILLIAMS (RV)** Marketing measures for information services. (Spec Libraries, 77; 1986; 61-70)

32. **ZAIS (HW):** Economic Modeling: An aid to Pricing of Information Services. (JASIS. 28; 1977; 89-95).

APPENDICES

APPENDIX I :
GUIDELINES : MARKETING OF INFORMATION SERVICES &PRODUCTS

The following guidelines were developed by ASTINFO at a Regional Workshop on Marketing of Information Services in Canberra, Australia, December 5 – 7, 1983.

INTRODUCTION

Information is used to help solve problems

Information is not a good in itself

Information is only of value when it is used

To make use of information, potential users must be aware of its existence.

THE CHALLENGE

Effective marketing is essential to the cost effective supply of information products and services.

The three stages of effective planning and marketing are:

1. Planning the marketing programme
2. Implementing the marketing programme
3. Auditing and evaluating the marketing programme

PLANNING THE MARKETING PROGRAMME

Preliminary Research	*Means*
What are our objectives?	
• Relation to institutional goals & policies	
• Private enterprise or public interest	Management Decision
• Reach as many people as possible, or thoroughly inform an elite few?	
What are our capabilities?	
• Set goals within achievable means	
Who are the potential / actual users for these capabilities?	Market Research
• Age, sex, location, socio-economic, educational standard, Racial or language background, organizational segment.	
What are the needs of high potential user groups?	
What benefits can we provide to these users?	

PLANNING THE PRODUCT

What are the highest potential product and/or market segments (user groups)?	Management Decision
What products and services could be marketed to these market segments?	Market Research
What is the most appropriate product mix for these market segments ?	
What price are they prepared to pay ?	
What are the critical factors in our operating environment that we need to consider in developing our marketing programme?	
• Which choices are ruled out through competition Legislation, supply source, or other uncontrollable External factors?	In-house

• Which are critical for development? (technological changes)	Research & Development
What product development is needed for these product / market segments?	
What delivery and distribution systems do these product / market segments require?	
What should be our budget, revenue and expenditure?	

PLANNING THE PROMOTIONAL PACKAGE

What promotional communication channels will be most effective in communicating with decision-makers and users in these potential product / market segments?	In-house or External Marketing
What is our marketing timetable?	Expertise
What capabilities do we need to establish and maintain these promotional channels?	Management Decision

MARKETING PLAN

What is our overall marketing plan?	Management
What period should this cover?	Decision

ASSESSING THE PROGRAMME

What will be the payback period for our initial investment in Marketing (including product development)	Financial
Can we market required products and services at a cost applicable to users and / or providers of funds?	Control
What are the priorities for available resource utilization?	Management
What will be the indirect impacts of our marketing programme?	Decision

What criteria will be used and how will we measure our performance against our objectives and plans?

Do we need to build into our programme any elements to assist in the later evaluation of the programme?

PRELIMINARY ACTIONS

Review marketing plan for practicality. If possible seek professional advice

ORGANISATION OF RESOURCES

Survey available resources including personnel, equipment supplies and communication channels.

Identify deficiencies in available resources

Determine finance requirements needed to meet resource deficiencies.

Recruit, reallocate, and retrain required staff

Develop, install or modify equipment necessary to provide product and / or service

Organise additional communication channels

Modify the programme as necessary to fit available resources (current plus obtainable additions)

EDUCATING AND TRAINING PROVIDERS OF FUNDS AND USERS OF SERVICE

Is there general awareness of products' existence?

Is equipment familiarization required?

Do new or modified techniques need to be taught?

Are communication methods understood?

What levels of product knowledge are required?

Is an awareness programme needed for providers of funds at two levels:

- Those who will decide if funds will be provided and if so, how much?
- Those in the funding organization who will use the service?

INTRODUCTORY TIMETABLE

Do we need to have time for a pilot programme? (Answer is almost - -yes)

What are the objectives of the pilot programme, e.g.

- Test promotional plan
- Test promotional channels
- Convince funding agencies

Has corrective action been taken as a result of pilot programme?

Are communication channels operating smoothly for:

- Awareness
- Product delivery

PROMOTIONAL MATERIAL

Establish budget

Identify, define and agree requirements

Establish target audience for promotional material agreed with plan

Keep image simple and relatable

Tailor promotional style to preferred media

If possible, pre-test promotional material

PROMOTIONAL CHANNELS

Identify appropriate channels having regard to the type of message, target audience and available finance. Channels include:

- TV
- Radio
- Print Media

- Seminars
- Exhibitions
- Workshops
- Demonstrations
- Posters
- Direct mail
- Luncheons
- Lectures

Don't overlook the obvious channels of:

- Over a sandwich in the office, or other contrived "Informal" contacts
- Social gatherings
- Videodiscs or tapes
- Stand-alone audio visuals

PRODUCT CHAMPIONS

Look for a product "champion" in your own organization

Identify and indoctrinate people who are willing to speak highly of the service.

A product champion:

- May not be the most visible person in the user organization
- Should be respected as a leader in product / service related discipline
- Must have credibility with the funding authority within their organization

DECISION MAKERS

Don't overlook the people who provide your funds: who they are, when you last communicated with them

Identify and wherever possible indoctrinate the person whose decision will be crucial to the use or otherwise of the service. (This may not be the person responsible for the organizational area using the product / service).

PROMOTIONAL PROGRAMME ONGOING MONITORING

Are the media being used still the most suitable?

Is the promotional material understood and digestible?

Are messages reaching the target group?

Identify likely adverse effects of programme.

Modify or stop programme as necessary.

Check to see revenue and costs are running in relation to budget and plan.

EVALUATING AND AUDITING THE MARKETING PROGRAMME

(The review stages of evaluation)

OBJECTIVES

What are the original objectives, regarding for instance:

PRODUCTS OR SERVICES

- Creating an awareness of availability of the product or service
- Sales / use of product or service
- Number of users
- Market share
- Profitability
- Expenditure
- Effective use of available resources
- Priorities between programmes

COMMUNITY INFORMATION PROGRAMMES

- Awareness
- Change or attitude

- Change of behavior
- Cost effectiveness

Have these objectives changed since we started the programme?

CRITERIA FOR MEASUREMENT OF PERFORMANCE AGAINST OBJECTIVES

What are the most relevant measures of performance (quantitative and qualitative)?

- Size of market and market share
- Number and value of sales
- Number of users
- Frequency of use by individual users
- Frequency of complaints
- User satisfaction regarding content, quality and timeliness
- User acceptance of charges
- Value for money from subsidies

What are the appropriate measures of promotional channel efficiency?

- Rate of increase in number of users
- Awareness by non-users
- "Distortion" introduced by the intermediaries in the service, or other channel inefficiencies and 'noise'.
- What are the indirect impact of your promotional campaign? e.g. Overload of document delivery service from promotion of on-line search capability.
- Profitability / costs of providing products / services
- Actual and comparison with budget
  - — Establishment costs
  - — Overheads
  - — Cost per unit of product
  - — Marginal cost per unit of product

CHANGE IN THE ENVIRONMENT

Have any changes in our environment outside our control affected our performance? E.g. technological change.

COMPETITION

Is the service losing or gaining market share?

Examine the reasons for this

- Poor product quality
- Slow delivery
- Changes in users' needs
- Competition: new types of services, better competitive marketing, and improved delivery systems

DATA NEEDS

What data are available for your evaluation?

- In-house statistics
- Data from external sources on market size and growth
- Competitor data
- Data from users

What additional data are needed?

How can these data be obtained? E.g. market research

What will be the cost of obtaining these data?

Is this cost justified?

If not justified, what else can be done?

RESULT OF EVALUATION

Have initial objectives been satisfied?

Were initial objectives realistic?

What are the reasons for any shortfall in performance?

What can be done to correct this shortfall?

- Product / service modification
- Promotional channels and programme
- Distribution system

Should marketing of this product or service be discontinued?

If not, how should product or service be altered or improved?

What changes are required to our marketing programme?

What is our plan and budget for our ongoing / amended marketing programme?

APPENDIX II : MODEL QUESTIONS

1. Define & discuss the concept of information with particular reference to it as a resource and a commodity.
2. What is marketing? Discuss the need and purpose of marketing information services & products.
3. Enumerate the differences between product-oriented & marketing approaches.
4. What are the objectives of marketing of information services?
5. Discuss the marketing concepts and the steps involved in a Marketing Programme.
6. List the barriers to adoption of marketing approach by information professionals.
7. List the steps involved in a marketing programme.
8. What is Marketing Strategy, especially in the context of Products?
9. Enumerate and explain the different marketing strategies that can be adopted by libraries.
10. Define Market research and discuss the stages and types of Market research.
11. What is Market Segmentation? Discuss the different strategies and methods of segmentation.
12. Define the term 'Marketing Mix' and briefly describe the components.
13. What is 'Marketing Communication? Discuss the different methods of Promotion.
14. Differentiate between traditional and digital marketing.
15. Discuss Market Segmentation in a digital environment.
16. What is Digital Marketing Mix? Discuss the components.

17. List the major pricing strategies
18. Discuss the concepts of Price and Pricing.
19. Describe the Pricing Strategies that can be adopted by Libraries and Information Centres.
20. Discuss the changing financial environment and scope for resource generation.
21. What are cost-recovery programmes and mention the points to be considered in such programmes.
22. Discuss the impact of pricing information services.
23. What are the demands and / or factors to be considered of Income Generating services?

APPENDIX III : GLOSSARY /KEY WORDS

Cost-Benefit Analysis : It is a technique that attempts to set out and evaluate the social cost and social benefits of investment projects to help decide whether or not a project should be undertaken.

Digital Marketing Mix : It consists of e-products, e-place, e-promotion, e- public relations and e-price.

Marginal Cost : The change in total cost of production, which results when output is varied by one unit.

Market Research : is the gathering together of all information at every level in the marketing process. It is putting into order the information that enables management to make better divisions

Market Segmentation : Is the act of dividing a market into meaningful parts or segments. Members of a particular segment are alike and different from members of other segments

Marketing : It is a planned approach to identifying and gaining the support of users and developing appropriate services in a manner, which benefits the users and furthers aims and objectives of the Library / Information Center.

Marketing Audit : It is an independent examination of the entire marketing effort of an Organisation covering objectives, programs, implementation, organization and control for the purpose of determining what is being done and recommending what should be done in the future.

Marketing Mix : It is the combination of product design, pricing, communication and distribution.

INDEX

AUTHOR INDEX

Note: Each entry consists of the name of the author followed by page Number(s).

SUBJECT INDEX

Note: Each entry consists of the name of the subject or kernel term followed by Page Number(s).

def = definition. *irt =in relation to*